barbecue bible

Parragon

This edition published by Parragon in 2009

Parragon
Queen Street House
4 Queen Street
Bath BA1 1HE
United Kingdom

This edition designed by Talking Design Ltd,
Worthing, West Sussex

Photography and text by The Bridgewater Book Company Ltd.

ISBN: 978-1-4075-7339-7

Printed in Indonesia

NOTE
This book uses metric and imperial measurements. Follow the same units of measurement
throughout; do not mix metric and imperial. All spoon measurements are level: teaspoons are
assumed to be 5 ml and tablespoons are assumed to be 15 ml. Unless otherwise stated, milk is
assumed to be full fat, eggs and individual vegetables such as potatoes are medium, and pepper is
freshly ground black pepper.

The times given for each recipe are an approximate guide only because the preparation times may
differ accordingly to the techniques used by different people and the cooking times may vary as a
result of the type of oven and other equipment used.

Recipes using raw or very lightly cooked eggs should be avoided by infants, the elderly, pregnant
women, convalescents and anyone suffering from an illness. Pregnant and breast-feeding women
are advised to avoid eating peanuts and peanut products.

contents

why BBQ?

In short, fun, friends and fine hearty food. Barbecuing is about delicious steaks or home-made burgers, fresh fish and colourful vegetables, and the sizzle and hiss of cooking in the background, merging with the bubble of conversation.

Good barbecuing means that the ritual of cooking is almost as important as the food itself. It is the one time that you can excuse blackened food and for once, taste rather than perfect presentation is the key.

A barbecue, when properly organised, can be one of the easiest, most sociable and most flexible of food activities. A barbecue can start early in the afternoon and stretch lazily into the evening. The smell of someone else's barbecue on a warm summer evening is all the incentive you should need!

basic barbecuing in ten easy steps

1.Choose your type of barbecue:
- Portable - light and easy to carry, ideal for a picnic if you are not walking too far.
- Disposable - made of a small foil tray with a wire rack and fuel supplied. They last up to an hour and can only be used once.
- Brazier - portable to a limited extent; some have legs and others have wheels, some also have a hood to protect the food.
- Gas/electric - expensive but very reliable; takes only 10 minutes to warm up, but does not produce the traditional smoky flavour.
- Kettle grill - with a hood, these are versatile and efficient. Some have a spit attachment.
- Permanent/custom-built - can be built into your garden, in the right spot and do not have to be expensive.

2.Choose your fuel:
- Lumpwood charcoal - easy to ignite, but will burn quite quickly. Inexpensive and easily available.
- Charcoal briquettes - can take a while to light, but burn for a long period with little smoke and smell.
- Self-igniting charcoal - is lumpwood charcoal or charcoal briquettes coated with a flammable chemical. Easy to light. Wait until the chemical has burned off before adding food to the rack.
- Hardwoods - such as oak and apple give a pleasant aroma and burn slowly. Soft woods are not an appropriate fuel.

3. Get your tools sorted - remember oven gloves and tongs to turn things over!

4. Pick your spot - if you are not using a fixed barbecue then be sure to choose a spot that is stable and on a flat surface. Don't move the barbecue once it's lit.

5. Preparation - use foil to line the base of your barbecue underneath the fire grate. This will make cleaning easier and will keep the bottom of the barbecue hot.

6. Set up your fuel - spread a layer of fuel on to the fire grate: small pieces at the bottom and medium-sized pieces on top of them works best. The layer of charcoal or wood should be 5cm/2 inches deep and resemble a pyramid in the centre of the grate (if you are using firelighters, see below).

7. Light the barbecue - if using firelighter cubes, place one or two in the centre of the pyramid. If using liquid firelighter, pour a few tablespoons in the fuel and leave for a minute. Never use petrol. Light the barbecue using a long match or taper and leave for 15 minutes. Remember to light your barbecue at least 1 hour before you want to start cooking.

8. Raising the temperature - spread the coals into an even layer and leave for 40 minutes, or until they are covered with a thin layer of grey ash and are hot enough to begin cooking. Spread the hot coals at least 2.5cm/1 inch further than the area on which you will be cooking the food.

9. **Controlling the barbecue -** to control the heat of the barbecue for cooking, raise or lower the grill rack. If your barbecue has air vents, open these to raise the temperature of the barbecue and close them to lower it. You can also push the hot coals carefully into the centre of the barbecue to provide a higher heat in the middle and a lower heat nearer the edges where you can put food once it is cooked.

10. **Cooking the food -** always make sure that food is thoroughly cooked through (see cooking times below). The barbecue needs to be very hot before you start cooking. Do not overcrowd food on the barbecue rack as individual pieces of food will not cook properly. Do not mix meat, vegetables and fish on the same rack. When cooking meat, turn steaks and burgers once, turn kebabs and sausages frequently. Brush the rack with a little sunflower oil (but not too much) to stop meat sticking.

Your complete guide to the finest ingredients

Beef
Cooking times
- Steaks 2.5 cm/1 inch thick should be cooked over hot coals for eight minutes. Cook for 5 minutes if you prefer steak rare, and for 12 minutes if you prefer it well done.
- Burgers 2 cm/ ³⁄₄ inch thick should be cooked over hot coals for 6-8 minutes.
- Kebabs made with medium-sized pieces of beef should be cooked for 7 minutes over hot coals.

Cuts of beef for barbecuing
Only the best cuts are suitable for barbecuing as it requires little cooking and has a superb taste. The majority of beef recipes in this book use:
- Sirloin - which is the tenderest cut from the back of the loin. It can be a large joint on the bone for roasting, but also provides tasty steaks for barbecuing.
- Rump steak - which comes from the hind quarter of the animal. It is thought to have the best flavour of all the steaks and can be cut into any size.

Other cuts of beef include:
- Fillet steak - which is the finest cut of beef: it is lean and boneless. It comes from below the sirloin and is the most expensive.
- Entrecôte steak - which is the lean and tender eye muscle of sirloin. It is also boneless, and can be cut into even-sized steaks, about 3-4cm/ 1¹⁄₄ - 1¹⁄₂ inches thick.
- T-bone - which is a steak from the thin end of the short loin containing a T-shaped bone and a piece of tenderloin.

Choosing red meat

Red meats should look fresh and moist but not too red. If the meat is bright red, it will not have hung long enough to develop a good flavour. A ruby/burgundy colour is better. The fat should be creamy rather than white. Trim fat from meat as excess fat dripping onto the coals could ignite.

Lamb
Cooking times

- Leg steaks should be cooked over medium hot coals for 10-15 minutes. If they are thicker than 2 cm/ ³/₄ inch, increase the cooking time or use a meat mallet to tenderise and flatten them a little.
- Chops 2.5 cm/1 inch thick are best cooked over medium hot coals for 15 minutes.
- Kebabs made with 2.5 cm/1 inch cubes of lamb should be cooked for about 8-15 minutes over medium hot coals.

Cuts of lamb for barbecuing

Recipes in this book include;
- Chump chops - which are smaller chops with a central bone.
- Rack of lamb - which is a very small joint, but is very tender. It is easy to carve by cutting down between the bones.
- Loin chops - which are cut from the loin and have a T-shaped bone.
- Fillet - which is a boneless strip of meat, cut from the middle neck. It is good cubed and made into kebabs for the barbecue.
- Steaks - which come from the top of the leg, also called gigot chops.
- Shoulder of lamb - which has a sweet flavour.
- Leg of lamb - which is a tender and lean joint.

Another cut of lamb is:

- Best end of neck cutlets - which are very small chops, cut from the best end of neck, with tender sweet meat and long, thin bones.

Pork
Cooking times

- Cook chops for 15-20 minutes over medium hot coals and make sure that they are cooked through. If they are thicker than 2.5 cm/1 inch, increase the cooking time accordingly.
- Kebabs made with 2.5 cm/1 inch cubes of pork should be cooked for about 15 minutes over medium hot coals.
- Most pork spare ribs are quite thick and will need to be cooked over medium hot coals for 40 minutes to ensure that they are cooked thoroughly.
- Thick sausages will need 10 minutes over medium hot coals; thinner ones may be ready slightly earlier.

Cuts of pork for barbecuing

Recipes in this book include:

- Spare ribs - which are cut from the thick end of belly pork.
- Fillet - which is also known as tenderloin and is very lean. It can also be cubed and made into kebabs.
- Chops - most recipes don't specify types of chops to be used, but for your information, loin chops are large lean chops with a good edge of fat that needs to be trimmed before barbecuing.

Choosing pork

Pork flesh should be smooth and moist and a pale pink colour. Organic pork will have a higher percentage of fat than factory pork (make sure this is trimmed before barbecuing) and will certainly have a better flavour. Sausages should contain at least 80% meat.

Chicken

Cooking times

- Quarters, legs and breasts with a bone should be cooked for 35 minutes over medium hot coals.
- Cook chicken drumsticks for 25-35 minutes over medium hot coals until the juices run clear, not pink, when you pierce the thickest part of the leg with a skewer or the point of a knife. If the drumsticks are very large, increase the cooking time.
- Whole breasts will need to be cooked over medium to hot coals for 15-20 minutes.
- Kebabs made with 2.5 cm/1 inch cubes of chicken should be cooked through after 10 minutes over medium hot coals.

Cuts of chicken for barbecuing

All chicken is suitable for barbecuing. The breasts are best if left on the bone because they will stay more moist. It is a good idea to marinate chicken pieces before cooking because this helps the meat stay moist while cooking.

Choosing chicken

Always try to use fresh chicken for barbecuing. Choose fresh birds that look soft, plump and creamy pink; they should not be scrawny, discoloured or bruised.

Fish and Seafood

Cooking times

- Cook whole small fish, up to 900 g/2 lb over medium hot coals for 5-7 minutes.
- Fish steaks, such as salmon or tuna, or fish fillets up to 2.5 cm/1 inch thick, should be cooked for 6-10 minutes over medium hot coals.
- Fish kebabs made with 2.5 cm/1 inch cubes of fish should be cooked over medium hot coals for 7 minutes.
- Prawns in their shells should be cooked over medium hot coals for 7 minutes if they are large. Smaller prawns should be threaded onto kebab skewers. Large shelled prawns will cook slightly faster.

Choosing fish and seafood

- If a fish or seafood has a "fishy odour" the product is already in decline and consequently will not taste pleasant.
- Gills should be deep red in colour, clean and clear of any mucus. Gills that are brown in colour suggest a lack of freshness.

- Raw prawns should be moist, firm and smell of the sea. Do not buy prawns that have either an ammonia smell or a fishy smell.
- Ask your fishmonger to gut whole fish, or take the head and tail off, if you wish.

Vegetables and Salads
Vegetables
You can barbecue nearly any vegetable. The best vegetables for barbecuing are aubergines, mushrooms, courgettes, peppers and corn on the cob. If you are cooking from raw, some vegetables do take a while to cook. There are individual recipes in this cookbook, but as a general rule you can speed up the process by parboiling vegetables indoors until they are nearly done.

Barbecue as follows:
- Brush with oil and sprinkle them with seasonings.
- Cook over medium hot coals. You can thread a variety of vegetables on skewers to make them easier to manage, or you can cut large vegetables in half and barbecue them individually.
- Turn the vegetables frequently, as they burn easily.

Salads
Of course, no barbecue would be complete without a deliciously crisp side salad. Fresh ingredients are the key to a fantastic salad and remember, if it is a hot day, don't leave your salad outside while you are cooking; keep it cool indoors until it is time to serve.

Choosing and preparing salad leaves
- When choosing salad greens look for firm leaves of good colour with no signs of browning or slime.
- They should be used within about two days of purchase, although very crisp lettuces, such as Iceberg and Little Gem can be stored in the salad drawer of the refrigerator for up to five days.
- Bags of mixed leaves are treated with oxygen to prolong their shelf life, but once the bag has been opened, they deteriorate very rapidly.
- To prepare, discard any coarse or wilted outer leaves and carefully wash the remainder in cold water. Drain well and then dry in a salad spinner or by wrapping them in a clean tea towel, as oil-based dressings will not adhere to wet leaves.

chargrilledburgers steaks mmmmflavour
glowing coals...

beef

steak with parsley butter

SERVES
2

PREP
5
mins

+2hrs
chilling

COOK
2-8
mins

The savoury herb butter in this recipe can be prepared well in advance and frozen, then used straight from the freezer to make this a very quick meal.

1 To make the Parsley Butter, put the butter in a small bowl and beat until it is smooth. Add the parsley and lemon juice with salt and cayenne pepper to taste and beat again until combined. Spoon the butter onto a piece of greaseproof paper and roll it into a sausage shape about 2.5 cm/1 inch thick. Chill in the refrigerator for 2 hours or until firm, or freeze for up to a month. Preheat the barbecue.

2 Rub a little butter on the steaks and then cook over hot coals for 1 minute on each side to brown. Move the rack up to reduce the temperature and season the steaks to taste with salt and pepper. Continue cooking for a further 2-3 minutes for rare; 4-5 minutes for medium; and 6-8 minutes for well done.

3 Transfer the steaks to warmed serving plates and spoon over the cooking juices from the pan. Cut the parsley butter into 6 thin slices and top each steak with 3 slices. Serve at once.

Ingredients

30 g/1 oz butter
1 tbsp sunflower oil
2 sirloin or rib-eye steaks, about 175 g/6 oz each and 2 cm/¾ inch thick, at room temperature
salt and pepper

for the parsley butter:
55 g/2 oz unsalted butter, softened
1½ tbsp very finely chopped fresh flat-leaf parsley
squeeze of lemon juice
salt
cayenne pepper

thai-spiced beef & pepper kebabs

 4 **20** +2½ hrs marinating **10-15**

This dish offers a spicy, flavoursome treat for a special barbecue party.

1 Put the sherry, rice wine, soy sauce, hoisin sauce, garlic, chilli, ginger and spring onions into a large bowl and mix until well combined. Season to taste.

2 Thread the meat onto 8 skewers, alternating it with chunks of red pepper. When the skewers are full (leave a small space at either end), transfer them to the bowl and turn them in the soy sauce mixture until they are well coated. Cover with clingfilm and place in the refrigerator to marinate for at least 2½ hours or overnight.

3 When the skewers are thoroughly marinated, lift them out and barbecue them over hot coals, turning them frequently, for 10–15 minutes or until the meat is cooked right through. Serve at once on a bed of green and red lettuce leaves.

italian steak melt burgers

SERVES
4

PREP
20
mins

+30 mins
chilling

COOK
8-13
mins

These delicious burgers will also be complemented by the use of cheeses such as mozzarella, fontina, Bel Paese or even Gorgonzola.

1 Place the steak mince, onion, garlic, red pepper, olives, pepper and tomato purée in a food processor and, using the pulse button, blend together. Shape into 4 equal-sized burgers, then cover and leave to chill for at least 30 minutes.

2 Place the burgers on a grill rack and cook over hot coals for 3-5 minutes on each side or until cooked to personal preference.

3 Place a tomato slice on top of each burger, then place the cheese over the tomato. Grill for a further 2–3 minutes, or until the cheese begins to melt. Serve.

ingredients

450 g/1 lb best steak mince
1 onion, grated
2–4 garlic cloves, crushed
1 small red pepper, deseeded, peeled and chopped
55 g/2 oz stoned black olives, finely chopped
pepper
1 tbsp tomato purée
2 large tomatoes, thickly sliced
85 g/3 oz Gruyère cheese, sliced

beef teriyaki

SERVES 4 **PREP 10 mins** **+2hrs marinating** **COOK 10-20 mins**

This Japanese-style teriyaki sauce complements beef, but it can also be used to accompany chicken or salmon.

1 Place the beef steaks in a shallow, non-metallic dish. To make the sauce, mix the cornflour and sherry together in a small bowl, then stir in the remaining sauce ingredients. Pour the sauce over the meat, cover with clingfilm and leave to marinate in the refrigerator for at least 2 hours.

2 Preheat the barbecue. Remove the meat from the sauce and reserve. Pour the sauce into a small saucepan and heat gently until it is just simmering, stirring occasionally.

3 Cut the meat into thin strips and thread these, concertina-style, on to several presoaked wooden skewers, alternating each strip of meat with the pieces of pepper and spring onion. Cook the kebabs over hot coals for 5–8 minutes, turning and basting the beef and vegetables occasionally with the reserved sauce.

4 Arrange the skewers on serving plates and pour over the remaining sauce. Serve with salad leaves.

ingredients

450 g/1 lb extra thin beef steaks
1 yellow pepper, deseeded and cut into chunks
8 spring onions, trimmed and cut into short lengths

sauce
1 tsp cornflour
2 tbsp dry sherry
2 tbsp white wine vinegar
3 tbsp soy sauce
1 tbsp dark muscovado sugar
1 garlic clove, crushed
$1/2$ tsp ground cinnamon
$1/2$ tsp ground ginger

to serve
salad leaves

ingredients

1 small onion, finely chopped
1 tbsp chopped fresh coriander
large pinch of paprika
$1/4$ tsp mixed spice
$1/4$ tsp ground coriander
$1/4$ tsp brown sugar
450 g/1 lb minced beef
salt and pepper
vegetable oil, for brushing

to garnish
fresh coriander leaves

to serve
freshly cooked bulgur wheat
 or rice
mixed salad

greek style beef kebabs

SERVES	PREP	COOK
4	**25** mins	**15-20** mins

Your barbecue party can take on a Greek theme with these tasty kebabs.

1 Put the onion, fresh coriander, spices, sugar and beef into a large bowl and mix until well combined. Season with salt and pepper.

2 On a clean work surface, use your hands to shape the mixture into sausages around skewers. Brush them lightly with vegetable oil.

3 Barbecue the kebabs over hot coals, turning them frequently, for 15–20 minutes or until cooked right through. Arrange the kebabs on a platter of freshly cooked bulgur wheat or rice and garnish with fresh coriander leaves. Serve with a mixed salad.

classic burger in a bun

SERVES
6

PREP
5
mins

+30 mins chilling

COOK
6-10
mins

This is a terrific meal for children – irresistible home-made burgers they can assemble themselves.

1 Put the minced steak, breadcrumbs, egg and thyme in a bowl and season with salt and pepper. Mix thoroughly, using your hands.

2 Divide the mixture into 6 portions and shape each into a round. Place on a plate, cover and chill for 30 minutes to firm up.

3 Cook the burgers over a medium barbecue for 3–5 minutes on each side, depending on how well done you like them. Turn them carefully as they will not be as firm as shop-bought burgers. Split the burger buns and toast them, cut side down, until golden. Place a burger in each bun and serve with a selection of fillings and accompaniments (well away from the barbecue fire).

ingredients

1 kg/2 lb 4 oz lean steak, minced
55 g/2 oz fresh breadcrumbs
1 egg, lightly beaten
1 tbsp chopped fresh thyme
salt and pepper

to serve
6 burger buns
lettuce leaves
red onion slices
tomato slices
dill pickle slices (optional)
tomato ketchup, relishes, mustard of choice

mustard steaks

SERVES **4**

PREP **10 mins**

+1hr cooling/ standing

COOK **50-60 mins**

Tarragon mustard gives these steaks a subtle spicy flavour that contrasts well with the sharp taste of the sweet-and-sour tomato relish.

1 To make the tomato relish, place all the ingredients in a heavy-based saucepan, seasoning to taste with salt. Bring to the boil, stirring, until the sugar has completely dissolved. Lower the heat and simmer, stirring occasionally, for 40 minutes or until thickened. Transfer to a bowl, cover with clingfilm and leave to cool.

2 Preheat the barbecue. Using a sharp knife, cut almost completely through each steak horizontally to make a pocket. Spread the mustard inside the pockets and rub the steaks all over with the garlic. Place the steaks on a plate, cover with clingfilm and leave to stand for 30 minutes.

3 Cook the steaks over hot coals for 2½ minutes each side for rare, 4 minutes each side for medium or 6 minutes each side for well done. Transfer to serving plates, garnish with fresh tarragon sprigs and serve immediately with the tomato relish.

ingredients

4 sirloin or rump steaks
1 tbsp tarragon mustard
2 garlic cloves, crushed

tomato relish
225 g/8 oz cherry tomatoes
55 g/2 oz Demerara sugar
50 ml/2 fl oz white wine
  vinegar
1 piece of stem ginger, chopped
½ lime, thinly sliced
salt

to garnish
sprigs of fresh tarragon

indonesian beef kebabs

SERVES **4**

PREP **15** mins

+2hrs marinating/ standing

COOK **10** mins

These spicy Indonesian kebabs are traditionally served with sambal kecap, a delicious chilli-flavoured dipping sauce.

1 To make the sauce, using a sharp knife, deseed the chilli and finely chop. Place in a small bowl with all the other sauce ingredients and mix together. Cover with clingfilm and leave to stand until required.

2 Dry-fry the coriander and cumin seeds in a frying pan for 1 minute, or until they give off their aroma and begin to pop. Remove from the heat and grind in a mortar with a pestle. Place the steak in a shallow, non-metallic dish and add the ground spices, stirring to coat. Put the onion, garlic, sugar, soy sauce and lemon juice into a food processor and process to a paste. Season to taste with salt and spoon the mixture over the steak, turning to coat. Cover with clingfilm and leave to marinate in the refrigerator for 2 hours.

3 Preheat the barbecue. Drain the steak, reserving the marinade, and thread it on to several presoaked wooden or metal skewers. Cook over hot coals, turning and basting frequently with the reserved marinade, for 5–8 minutes, until thoroughly cooked. Transfer to a large serving plate and serve with the sauce for dipping.

ingredients

1 tsp coriander seeds
1/2 tsp cumin seeds
450 g/1 lb rump steak
 cut into strips
1 onion
2 garlic cloves
1 tbsp muscovado sugar
1 tbsp dark soy sauce
4 tbsp lemon juice
salt

sauce
1 fresh red chilli
4 tbsp dark soy sauce
2 garlic cloves, finely chopped
4 tsp lemon juice
2 tbsp hot water

rump steak with dark barbecue sauce

SERVES	PREP		COOK
6	**10** mins	**+4hrs** marinating	**30–35** mins

This barbecue favourite is marinated in a spicy sauce and served with a topping of shallot butter.

1 Heat the oil in a large frying pan. Cook the onion over a low heat, stirring occasionally, for 5 minutes, or until softened. Stir in the tomatoes, lemon juice, Tabasco and Worcestershire sauces, sugar and mustard powder. Cover and simmer, stirring occasionally, for 15–20 minutes, or until thickened. Pour into a large dish and leave to cool.

2 Meanwhile, blanch the shallots in boiling water for 2–3 minutes. Drain well and pat dry with kitchen paper. Place in a food processor and process to a purée. Gradually work in the butter and season with salt and pepper. Scrape the shallot butter into a bowl, cover and chill until required.

3 Add the steaks to the cooled marinade, turning to coat. Cover and marinate in a cool place for 4 hours.

4 Drain the steaks, reserving the marinade. Grill on a hot barbecue, brushing frequently with the marinade, for 2 minutes on each side for rare, 4 minutes on each side for medium or 6 minutes on each side for well done. Serve each steak topped with a spoonful of shallot butter and garnish with watercress sprigs.

ingredients

2 tbsp sunflower oil

marinade
1 onion, finely chopped
450 g/1 lb tomatoes, peeled, deseeded and chopped
2 tbsp lemon juice
1 tbsp Tabasco sauce
2 tbsp Worcestershire sauce
2 tbsp muscovado sugar
1 tsp mustard powder
140 g/5 oz shallots, finely chopped
140 g/5 oz butter, softened
6 rump steaks, about 175 g/6 oz each
salt and pepper

to garnish
few sprigs of watercress

new orleans steak sandwich

SERVES **4** PREP **10-12** mins COOK **30-35** mins

An aristocratic relation of the humble burger, this is a positive feast for serious meat eaters.

ingredients

4 tbsp olive oil
2 large onions, sliced thinly
  into rings
2 garlic cloves, chopped
1 tbsp red wine vinegar
1 tbsp chopped fresh thyme
3 tbsp chopped fresh parsley
2 tsp prepared mild mustard
salt and pepper
4 rump steaks, about 175 g/
  6 oz each
8 slices sourdough or crusty
  bread
115 g/4 oz Roquefort cheese,
  crumbled
4 tomatoes, sliced
1 Little Gem lettuce, shredded

1 Heat half the oil in a heavy-based frying pan. Add the onions and garlic, sprinkle with a pinch of salt, then cover and cook over a very low heat for 25–30 minutes, or until very soft and caramelized.

2 Process the onion mixture in a food processor until smooth. Scrape into a bowl, stir in the vinegar, thyme, parsley and mustard and season with salt and pepper. Cover and place at the side of the barbecue.

3 Brush the steaks with the remaining oil and season with salt and pepper. Grill on a hot barbecue for 2 minutes on each side for rare, 4 minutes on each side for medium or 6 minutes on each side for well done.

4 Meanwhile, toast the bread on both sides. Spread the onion mixture on the toast. Slice the steaks and top 4 toast slices with the meat. Sprinkle with the crumbled Roquefort, then add the tomatoes and lettuce leaves. Top with the remaining toast and serve.

beef satay

SERVES
6

PREP
10
mins

+2hrs
marinating

COOK
5-8
mins

The term 'satay' refers to a kebab that has been marinated in a flavoursome mixture of any kind and is not just a reference to a peanut sauce.

1 Using a sharp knife, cut the steak into 2.5-cm/1-inch cubes, then place in a large, shallow, non-metallic dish. Mix the honey, soy sauce, oil, garlic, coriander, caraway seeds and chilli powder together in a small jug. Pour the mixture over the steak and stir until the steak is thoroughly coated with the marinade. Cover with clingfilm and leave to marinate in the refrigerator for 2 hours, turning occasionally.

2 Preheat the barbecue. Drain the steak, reserving the marinade. Thread the steak on to several presoaked wooden skewers.

3 Cook the steak over hot coals, turning and brushing frequently with the reserved marinade, for 5–8 minutes. Transfer to a large serving plate, garnish with lime wedges and serve.

ingredients

1 kg/2 lb 4 oz rump steak
1 tbsp clear honey
2 tbsp dark soy sauce
2 tbsp groundnut oil
1 garlic clove, finely chopped
1 tsp ground coriander
1 tsp caraway seeds
pinch of chilli powder

to garnish
lime wedges

beefburgers with chilli and basil

| SERVES 4 | PREP 10 mins | COOK 10-16 mins |

A tasty traditional barbecue dish – with an extra spiciness.

1 Put the minced beef, red pepper, garlic, chillies, chopped basil and cumin into a bowl and mix until well combined. Season with salt and pepper.

2 Using your hands, form the mixture into burger shapes. Barbecue the burgers over hot coals for 5–8 minutes on each side, or until cooked right through. Garnish with sprigs of basil and serve in hamburger buns.

ingredients

650 g/1 lb 7 oz minced beef
1 red pepper, deseeded and
  finely chopped
1 garlic clove, finely chopped
2 small red chillies, deseeded
  and finely chopped
1 tbsp chopped fresh basil
1/2 tsp powdered cumin
salt and pepper

to garnish
sprigs of fresh basil

to serve
hamburger buns

middle eastern koftas

SERVES	PREP	COOK
4	**10** mins	**10** mins

For a twist to the normal barbecue kebab try these koftas which
are quick and easy to make and taste delicious.

1 Blend the meat, onion, garlic, parsley, spices and seasoning to a smooth paste in a food processor. Turn into a large mixing bowl.

2 Select flat skewers that fit comfortably onto your barbecue rack.

3 Take about 2 tablespoons of meat paste and roll gently between your palms to make a sausage shape. Carefully fold around the skewer. If you cannot find flat skewers, shape the meat into patties as you would for hamburgers.

4 Brush the koftas with minted yoghurt marinade and cook over hot coals for 10 minutes, turning carefully and basting regularly.

5 When the meat is cooked, transfer to a large serving platter and garnish with sprigs of fresh mint and lemon wedges. Serve with rice or Indian bread and bowls of cucumber yogurt raita and tomato onion salad.

ingredients

750 g/1 lb 10 oz minced
 lamb or beef
1 small onion, quartered
2 garlic cloves, crushed
2 tbsp chopped fresh
 flat-leaf parsley
1 tsp coriander seeds
$1/2$ tsp cumin seeds
$1/2$ tsp whole black peppercorns
generous pinch of ground
 cinnamon
pinch of salt
Minted Yogurt Marinade
 (see page 218)

to garnish
fresh mint and lemon wedges

serving suggestions
rice or Indian bread
cucumber yogurt raita
tomato and onion salad

cheese and apple burgers

SERVES **4-6**

PREP **10-12** mins

+30 mins chilling

COOK **12-18** mins

ingredients

450 g/1 lb best steak mince
1 onion, finely chopped
1–2 tsp wholegrain mustard,
  or to taste
pepper
2–3 tsp Worcestershire sauce
55 g/2 oz mature Cheddar
  cheese, grated
2 Bramley cooking apples
1 tsp butter, melted
2–3 tsp caster sugar
55 g/2 oz Gruyère cheese,
  thinly sliced

Savoury cheese and sweet apple unite in this magic burger, adding melting texture and sharp flavour to the tender beef.

1 Preheat the barbecue. Place the steak mince in a large bowl. Add the onion, mustard, pepper, Worcestershire sauce to taste and the grated cheese. Peel and core 1 of the apples, then grate and add to the bowl. Mix together, then shape into 4 equal-sized burgers. Cover and leave to chill for 30 minutes.

2 Preheat the grill to medium-high. Peel and core the remaining apple whole, then cut into 4–6 thick slices. Brush with the melted butter and sprinkle with the caster sugar. Place on a foil-lined grill rack and cook under the hot grill for 2–3 minutes on each side or until caramelized. Reserve.

3 Cook the burgers over hot coals for 4-6 minutes on each side or until cooked to personal preference. Top the burgers with the sliced cheese and continue to cook until the cheese has melted. Serve.

chopsizzlesausageribssensationalsauces
meatballstasty...

pork

sausages with barbecue sauce

SERVES	PREP	COOK
4	5-8 mins	30-35 mins

Although there is much more to barbecues than sausages, they can make a welcome appearance from time to time.

1 To make the sauce, heat the oil in a small pan and fry the onion and garlic for 4–5 minutes until softened and just beginning to brown.

2 Add the tomatoes, Worcestershire sauce, brown fruity sauce, sugar, wine vinegar, chilli powder, mustard powder, Tabasco sauce and salt and pepper to taste to the pan and bring to the boil.

3 Reduce the heat and simmer gently for 10–15 minutes until the sauce begins to thicken slightly. Stir occasionally so that the sauce does not burn and stick to the bottom of the pan. Set aside and keep warm until required.

4 Barbecue the sausages over hot coals for 10–15 minutes, turning frequently. Do not prick them with a fork or the juices and fat will run out and cause the barbecue to flare.

5 Insert the sausages into the bread rolls and serve with the barbecue sauce.

ingredients

2 tbsp sunflower oil
1 large onion, chopped
2 cloves garlic, chopped
225 g/8 oz can chopped tomatoes
1 tbsp Worcestershire sauce
2 tbsp brown fruity sauce
2 tbsp light muscovado sugar
4 tbsp white wine vinegar
$1/2$ tsp mild chilli powder
$1/4$ tsp mustard powder
dash of Tabasco sauce
450 g/1 lb sausages
salt and pepper

to serve
bread finger rolls

chinese ribs

SERVES	PREP		COOK
4	**10** mins	**+6hrs** marinating	**30–40** mins

Marinate for as long as possible to ensure that the wonderful flavours of the marinade permeate the meat.

ingredients

1 kg/2 lb 4 oz pork spare
  ribs, separated
4 tbsp dark soy sauce
3 tbsp muscovado sugar
1 tbsp groundnut or sunflower oil
2 garlic cloves, finely chopped
2 tsp Chinese five-spice powder
1-cm/^{1}/$_2$-inch piece fresh root
  ginger, grated

to garnish
shredded spring onions

1 Place the spare ribs in a large, shallow, non-metallic dish. Mix the soy sauce, sugar, oil, garlic, Chinese five-spice powder and ginger together in a bowl. Pour the mixture over the ribs and turn until the ribs are thoroughly coated in the marinade.

2 Cover the dish with clingfilm and leave to marinate in the refrigerator for at least 6 hours.

3 Preheat the barbecue. Drain the ribs, reserving the marinade. Cook over medium hot coals, turning and brushing frequently with the reserved marinade, for 30–40 minutes. Transfer to a large serving dish, garnish with the shredded spring onions and serve immediately.

pork burgers with tangy orange marinade

SERVES	PREP		COOK
4-6	12 mins	+1hr marinating/ chilling	26-30 mins

The large pieces of orange peel in the marmalade play their part by adding extra texture to this burger.

1 Place the pork in a shallow dish. Place the marmalade, orange juice and vinegar in a small saucepan and heat, stirring, until the marmalade has melted. Pour the marinade over the pork. Cover and leave for at least 30 minutes, or longer if time permits. Remove the pork, reserving the marinade. Mince the pork into a large bowl.

2 Meanwhile, cook the parsnips in a saucepan of boiling water for 15–20 minutes, or until cooked. Drain, then mash and add to the pork. Stir in the orange rind, garlic, spring onions, courgette and salt and pepper to taste. Mix together, then shape into 4–6 equal-sized burgers. Cover and leave to chill for at least 30 minutes.

3 Preheat the barbecue. Lightly brush each burger with a little oil and then add them to the barbecue grill, cooking over medium hot coals for 4-6 minutes on each side or until thoroughly cooked. Boil the reserved marinade for 3 minutes, then pour into a small jug or bowl. Serve.

ingredients

450 g/1 lb pork fillet, cut into
  small pieces
3 tbsp Seville orange marmalade
2 tbsp orange juice
1 tbsp balsamic vinegar
225 g/8 oz parsnips,
  cut into chunks
1 tbsp finely grated orange rind
2 garlic cloves, crushed
6 spring onions, finely chopped
1 courgette (175 g/6 oz), grated
salt and pepper
1 tbsp sunflower oil

normandy brochettes

SERVES	PREP	+1-2 hrs marinating	COOK
4	**10** mins		**12-15** mins

The orchards of Normandy are famous throughout France, providing both eating apples and cider-making varieties.

ingredients

450 g/1 lb pork fillet
300 ml/10 fl oz dry cider
1 tbsp finely chopped fresh sage
6 black peppercorns, crushed
2 crisp eating apples
1 tbsp sunflower oil

1 Using a sharp knife, cut the pork into 2.5-cm/1-inch cubes, then place in a large, shallow, non-metallic dish. Mix the cider, sage and peppercorns together in a jug, pour the mixture over the pork and turn until thoroughly coated. Cover with clingfilm and leave to marinate in the refrigerator for 1–2 hours.

2 Preheat the barbecue. Drain the pork, reserving the marinade. Core the apples, but do not peel, then cut into wedges. Dip the apple wedges into the reserved marinade and thread on to several metal skewers, alternating with the cubes of pork. Stir the sunflower oil into the remaining marinade.

3 Cook the brochettes over medium hot coals, turning and brushing frequently with the reserved marinade, for 12–15 minutes. Transfer to a large serving plate and if you prefer, remove the meat and apples from the skewers before serving. Serve immediately.

hot & spicy ribs

ingredients

1 onion, chopped
2 garlic cloves, chopped
2.5-cm/1-inch piece fresh root
  ginger, sliced
1 fresh red chilli, deseeded
  and chopped
5 tbsp dark soy sauce
3 tbsp lime juice
1 tbsp palm or muscovado sugar
2 tbsp groundnut oil
salt and pepper
1 kg/2 lb 4 oz pork spare ribs,
  separated

SERVES	PREP	COOK
4	15 mins	1 hr

These succulent pork spare ribs are deliciously tender and packed full of spicy flavours.

1 Preheat the barbecue. Put the onion, garlic, ginger, chilli and soy sauce into a food processor and process to a paste. Transfer to a jug and stir in the lime juice, sugar and oil and season to taste with salt and pepper.

2 Place the spare ribs in a preheated wok or large, heavy-based saucepan and pour in the soy sauce mixture. Place on the hob and bring to the boil, then simmer over a low heat, stirring frequently, for 30 minutes. If the mixture appears to be drying out, add a little water.

3 Remove the spare ribs, reserving the sauce. Cook the ribs over medium hot coals, turning and basting frequently with the sauce, for 20–30 minutes. Transfer to a large serving plate and serve immediately.

047

barbecued pork sausages with thyme

SERVES	PREP	+45	COOK
4	**15** mins	**mins** chilling	**15** mins

These sausages will make you rediscover the variety and joy of one of the best-loved barbecue foods.

1 Put the garlic, onion, chilli, pork, almonds, breadcrumbs and fresh thyme into a large bowl. Season well with salt and pepper and mix until well combined.

2 Using your hands, form the mixture into sausage shapes. Roll each sausage in a little flour, then transfer to a bowl, cover with clingfilm and refrigerate for 45 minutes.

3 Brush a piece of aluminium foil with oil, then put the sausages on the foil and brush them with a little more vegetable oil. Transfer the sausages and foil to the barbecue. Barbecue over hot coals, turning the sausages frequently, for about 15 minutes or until cooked right through. Serve with finger rolls, cooked sliced onion and tomato ketchup and/or mustard.

ingredients

1 garlic clove, finely chopped
1 onion, grated
1 small red chilli, deseeded and finely chopped
450 g/1 lb lean minced pork
50 g/1³/₄ oz almonds, toasted and ground
50 g/1³/₄ oz fresh breadcrumbs
1 tbsp finely chopped fresh thyme
salt and pepper
flour, for dusting
vegetable oil, for brushing

to serve
fresh finger rolls
slices of onion, lightly cooked
tomato ketchup and/or mustard

pork & sage kebabs

MAKES 12

PREP 10-15 mins

+30 mins chilling

COOK 8-10 mins

These kebabs have a delicious, slightly sweet flavour that is popular with children.

1 Place the mince in a mixing bowl together with the breadcrumbs, onion, sage, apple sauce, nutmeg and salt and pepper to taste. Mix until the ingredients are well combined.

2 Using your hands, shape the mixture into small balls, about the size of large marbles, and leave to chill in the refrigerator for at least 30 minutes.

3 Meanwhile, soak 12 small wooden skewers in cold water for at least 30 minutes. Thread the meatballs on to the skewers.

4 To make the baste, mix together the oil and lemon juice in a small bowl, whisking with a fork until it is well blended.

5 Barbecue the kebabs over hot coals for 8–10 minutes, turning and basting frequently with the lemon and oil mixture, until the meat is golden and cooked through.

6 Line the pitta breads with the salad leaves and spoon over some of the yogurt. Serve with the kebabs.

ingredients

450 g/1 lb pork mince
25 g/1 oz fresh breadcrumbs
1 small onion, chopped
  very finely
1 tbsp fresh sage, chopped
2 tbsp apple sauce
$1/4$ tsp ground nutmeg
salt and pepper

baste
3 tbsp olive oil
1 tbsp lemon juice

to serve
6 small pitta breads
mixed salad leaves
6 tbsp thick, natural yogurt

meatballs on sticks

SERVES
8

PREP
20
mins

COOK
10
mins

ingredients

4 pork and herb sausages
115 g/4 oz fresh beef mince
85 g/3 oz fresh white
  breadcrumbs
1 onion, finely chopped
2 tbsp chopped mixed
  fresh herbs, such as parsley,
  thyme and sage
1 egg
salt and pepper
sunflower oil, for brushing

to serve
sauces of your choice

To cater for all palates, serve with a selection of ready-made or home-made sauces.

1 Preheat the barbecue. Remove the sausage meat from the skins, place in a large bowl and break up with a fork. Add the beef mince, breadcrumbs, onion, herbs and egg. Season to taste with salt and pepper and stir well with a wooden spoon until thoroughly mixed.

2 Form the mixture into small balls, about the size of a golf ball, between the palms of your hands. Spear each one with a cocktail stick and brush with oil.

3 Cook over medium hot coals, turning frequently and brushing with more oil as necessary, for 10 minutes, or until cooked through. Transfer to a large serving plate and serve immediately with a choice of sauces.

pork medallions with grilled apples

SERVES	PREP	+8-12	COOK
4	**15-20** mins	**hrs** marinating	**40-45** mins

This tasty chargrilled treat needs to be served with no more than a mixed salad and some crusty bread.

1 Make the marinade. Heat the oil and cook the garlic and shallots over a low heat, stirring occasionally, for 5 minutes, until soft. Stir in the remaining marinade ingredients and simmer gently for 5 minutes. Remove from the heat and leave to cool completely.

2 Cut the pork fillet into medallions about 1 cm/^{1}/$_2$ inch thick and place in a shallow dish. Pour in the marinade, turning to coat. Cover with clingfilm and marinate in the refrigerator overnight.

3 With a sharp knife, score through the skin of each apple around the centre. Place each apple on a square of foil and put a rosemary sprig and 1 tsp sugar in each cavity. Enclose the apples in the foil and cook on a medium barbecue, turning occasionally, for 25–30 minutes.

4 About 10–15 minutes before the apples are ready, drain the pork, reserving the marinade. Grill, brushing with the reserved marinade for about 5 minutes on each side. Put 3–4 medallions on each plate with an unwrapped apple. Garnish with extra rosemary sprigs and serve.

ingredients

500 g/1 lb 2 oz pork fillet
4 eating apples, cored
4 small rosemary sprigs, plus extra to garnish
4 tsp caster sugar

marinade

2 tbsp olive oil
1 garlic clove, finely chopped
4 shallots, finely chopped
4 tbsp orange juice
2 tbsp clear honey
1 tbsp Worcestershire sauce
1 tsp Dijon mustard
3 tbsp white wine vinegar
1 rosemary sprig, finely chopped

pigs in blankets

SERVES	PREP	COOK
4	15 mins	15–20 mins

This recipe transforms barbecue sausages into a dish that is fun and delicious.

1 Preheat the barbecue. Thinly slice the mozzarella cheese. Cut a deep slit in the side of each sausage, using a sharp knife. Spread the cut sides with the mustard. Divide the slices of cheese between the sausages and reshape them.

2 Stretch the bacon with a heavy, flat-bladed knife. Wrap 1 bacon rasher tightly around each sausage to hold it together. If necessary, secure with a cocktail stick.

3 Cook over hot coals, turning frequently, for 15–20 minutes. Transfer to a large serving plate and serve immediately.

ingredients

115 g/4 oz mozzarella cheese
8 Toulouse sausages
2 tbsp Dijon mustard
8 smoked bacon rashers

ingredients

400 g/14 oz lean pork fillet
3 tbsp orange marmalade
grated rind and juice of 1 orange
1 tbsp white wine vinegar
dash of Tabasco sauce
salt and pepper

sauce
1 tbsp olive oil
1 small onion, chopped
1 small green pepper, deseeded and
  thinly sliced
1 tbsp cornflour
150 ml/5 fl oz orange juice

to serve
cooked rice
mixed salad leaves

tangy pork fillet

SERVES	PREP	COOK
4	10 mins	55 mins

Barbecued in a parcel of kitchen foil, these tasty pork fillets are served with a tangy orange sauce.

1 Place a large piece of double thickness foil in a shallow dish. Put the pork fillet in the centre of the foil and season.

2 Heat the marmalade, orange rind and juice, vinegar and Tabasco sauce in a small pan, stirring until the marmalade melts and the ingredients combine. Pour the mixture over the pork and wrap the meat in foil, making sure that the parcel is well sealed so that the juices cannot run out. Place over hot coals and barbecue for about 25 minutes, turning the parcel occasionally.

3 For the sauce, heat the oil and cook the onion for 2–3 minutes. Add the pepper and cook for 3–4 minutes.

4 Remove the pork from the kitchen foil and place on to the rack. Pour the juices into the pan with the sauce.

5 Barbecue the pork for a further 10–20 minutes, turning, until cooked through and golden on the outside.

6 In a small bowl, mix the cornflour with a little orange juice to form a paste. Add to the sauce with the remaining cooking juices. Cook, stirring, until the sauce thickens. Slice the pork, spoon over the sauce and serve with rice and mixed salad leaves.

frankly fabulous skewers

SERVES	PREP	COOK
4	**10** mins	**40** mins

A new way with an old favourite – cook frankfurter sausages on the barbecue for a great smoky flavour and a very easy meal.

ingredients

12 frankfurter sausages
2 courgettes, cut into
  1-cm/^{1}/$_2$-inch slices
2 corn cobs, cut into
  1-cm/^{1}/$_2$-inch slices
12 cherry tomatoes
12 baby onions
2 tbsp olive oil

garlic toast
2 garlic bulbs
2–3 tbsp olive oil
1 baguette, sliced
salt and pepper

1 Preheat the barbecue. To make the garlic toast, slice off the tops of the garlic bulbs. Brush the bulbs with oil and wrap them in foil. Cook over hot coals, turning occasionally, for 30 minutes.

2 Meanwhile, cut each frankfurter sausage into 3 pieces. Thread the frankfurter pieces, courgette slices, corn cob slices, cherry tomatoes and baby onions alternately on to metal skewers. Brush with olive oil.

3 Cook the skewers over hot coals, turning and brushing frequently with the oil, for 8–10 minutes. Meanwhile, brush the slices of baguette with oil and toast both sides on the barbecue. Unwrap the garlic bulbs and squeeze the cloves on to the bread. Season to taste with salt and pepper and drizzle over a little extra olive oil, if you like. Transfer the skewers to a large serving plate and serve immediately with the garlic toast.

soy pork with coriander

SERVES	PREP		COOK
4	**10** mins	**+1hr** marinating	**14-20** mins

The spicy, Eastern-style flavours that suffuse these pork chops will make them an unusual and original barbecue favourite.

1 Place the pork chops in a large, shallow, non-metallic dish. Crush the coriander seeds and peppercorns in a spice mill. Alternatively, place in a mortar and crush with a pestle. Place the soy sauce, garlic, sugar, crushed coriander seeds and peppercorns in a jug and stir well until the sugar has dissolved.

2 Pour the soy sauce mixture over the chops, turning to coat. Cover with clingfilm and leave to marinate in the refrigerator for 1 hour, turning occasionally.

3 Preheat the barbecue. Drain the chops, reserving the marinade. Cook over medium hot coals, brushing frequently with the reserved marinade, for 7–10 minutes on each side. Transfer to a large serving plate, garnish with fresh coriander sprigs and serve.

ingredients

4 pork chops, about 175 g/
  6 oz each
1 tbsp coriander seeds
6 black peppercorns
4 tbsp dark soy sauce
1 garlic clove, finely chopped
1 tsp sugar

to garnish
fresh coriander sprigs

herbed pork chops with blue cheese and walnut butter

SERVES	PREP		COOK
4	**10** mins	**+12 hrs** marinating	**35–40** mins

The flavoured butter adds a wonderfully rich taste to the barbecued chops as it melts.

1 Trim the fat from the chops and place them in a dish. Whisk together the oil, lemon juice, marjoram, thyme, parsley, garlic and onion in a bowl, then season with salt and pepper. Pour the marinade over the chops, turning to coat. Cover and marinate in the refrigerator overnight.

2 To make the flavoured butter, melt half the butter in a frying pan and cook the spring onions over a low heat, stirring frequently for a few minutes, until softened. Transfer to a bowl and mix in the remaining butter, the cheese and walnuts. Form into a roll, then cover and chill until required.

3 Drain the chops, reserving the marinade. Grill the chops on a hot barbecue for 5 minutes on each side, then grill over more medium coals or on a higher rack, turning and brushing occasionally with the reserved marinade, for about 10 minutes more on each side, or until cooked through and tender. Transfer to serving plates and top each chop with 1–2 slices of the cheese and walnut butter. Serve immediately with a small salad.

ingredients

4 pork chops

marinade
4 tbsp sunflower oil
2 tbsp lemon juice
1 tbsp chopped fresh marjoram
1 tbsp chopped fresh thyme
2 tablespoons chopped fresh
  parsley
1 garlic clove, finely chopped
1 onion, finely chopped
salt and pepper

blue cheese and walnut butter
55 g/2 oz butter
4 spring onions, finely chopped
140 g/5 oz dolcelatte cheese,
  crumbled
2 tbsp finely chopped walnuts

to serve
small salad

pork & apple skewers

SERVES	PREP	COOK
4	10 mins	15 mins

Flavoured with mustard and served with a mustard sauce, these kebabs make an ideal lunch.

1 To make the mustard sauce, combine the wholegrain and Dijon mustards in a small bowl and slowly blend in the cream. Leave to stand until required.

2 Cut the pork fillet into bite-size pieces and set aside until required.

3 Core the apples, then cut them into thick wedges. Toss the apple wedges in a little lemon juice – this will prevent any discoloration. Slice the lemon.

4 Thread the pork, apple and lemon slices alternately on to 4 metal or pre-soaked wooden skewers.

5 Mix together the mustards, apple or orange juice and sunflower oil. Brush the mixture over the kebabs and barbecue over hot coals for 10–15 minutes, until cooked through, frequently turning and basting the kebabs with the mustard marinade.

6 Transfer the kebabs to warm serving plates and spoon over a little of the mustard sauce. Serve the kebabs with fresh, crusty brown bread.

ingredients

450 g/1 lb pork fillet
2 eating apples
a little lemon juice
1 lemon
2 tsp wholegrain mustard
2 tsp Dijon mustard
2 tbsp apple or orange juice
2 tbsp sunflower oil

mustard sauce
1 tbsp wholegrain mustard
1 tsp Dijon mustard
6 tbsp single cream

to serve
crusty brown bread

kebab**tasty**tangy**sumptuous**fillet**juicy**
brochettetender...

lamb

minted lamb chops

SERVES 6

PREP 15 mins

+2hrs marinating

COOK 10-14 mins

You can prepare this dish with any kind of lamb chops, however, shoulder steaks also work well.

1 Place the chops in a large, shallow, non-metallic bowl. Mix half the yogurt, the garlic, ginger and coriander seeds together in a jug and season to taste with salt and pepper. Spoon the mixture over the chops, turning to coat, then cover with clingfilm and leave to marinate in the refrigerator for 2 hours, turning occasionally.

2 Preheat the barbecue. Place the remaining yogurt, the olive oil, orange juice, walnut oil and mint in a small bowl and, using a hand-held whisk, whisk until thoroughly blended. Season to taste with salt and pepper. Cover the minted yogurt with clingfilm and leave to chill in the refrigerator until ready to serve.

3 Drain the chops, scraping off the marinade. Brush with olive oil and cook over medium hot coals for 5–7 minutes on each side. Serve immediately with the minted yogurt.

ingredients

6 chump chops, about 175 g/
  6 oz each
150 ml/5 fl oz natural Greek
  yogurt
2 garlic cloves, finely chopped
1 tsp grated fresh root ginger
$^1/_4$ tsp coriander seeds, crushed
salt and pepper
1 tbsp olive oil, plus extra
  for brushing
1 tbsp orange juice
1 tsp walnut oil
2 tbsp chopped fresh mint

moroccan lamb kebabs

SERVES	PREP	+2-8 hrs	COOK
4	25 mins	marinating	10 mins

Marinated in Moroccan spices, these barbecued kebabs have a mild spicy flavour. Add the chilli if you like a bit of zip to your meat.

ingredients

450 g/1 lb lean lamb
1 lemon
1 red onion
4 small courgettes

marinade
grated rind and juice of 1 lemon
2 tbsp olive oil
1 clove garlic, crushed
1 red chilli, sliced (optional)
1 tsp ground cinnamon
1 tsp ground ginger
$^1/_2$ tsp ground cumin
$^1/_2$ tsp ground coriander

to serve
couscous

1 Cut the lamb into large, evenly-sized chunks.

2 To make the marinade, combine the lemon rind and juice, oil, garlic, chilli (if using), ground cinnamon, ginger, cumin and coriander in a large non-metallic dish.

3 Add the meat to the marinade, tossing to coat the meat completely. Cover and leave to marinate in the refrigerator for at least 2 hours or preferably overnight.

4 Cut the lemon into 8 pieces. Cut the onion into wedges, then separate each wedge into 2 pieces.

5 Using a potato peeler, cut thin strips of peel from the courgettes, then cut the courgettes into chunks.

6 Remove the meat from the marinade, reserving the liquid for basting. Thread the meat on to skewers alternating with the onion, lemon and courgette.

7 Barbecue over hot coals for 8–10 minutes, turning and basting with the reserved marinade. Serve on a bed of couscous.

rack & ruin

SERVES	PREP		COOK
4	10 mins	**+1hr** marinating	20 mins

This quick and easy dish is perfect for serving as part of a summer party menu, along with plenty of salad and potatoes.

1 Place the racks of lamb in a large, shallow, non-metallic dish. Place the oil, vinegar, lemon juice, rosemary and onion in a jug and stir together. Season to taste with salt and pepper.

2 Pour the marinade over the lamb and turn until thoroughly coated. Cover with clingfilm and leave to marinate in the refrigerator for 1 hour, turning occasionally.

3 Preheat the barbecue. Drain the racks of lamb, reserving the marinade. Cook over medium hot coals, brushing frequently with the marinade, for 10 minutes on each side. Serve immediately.

ingredients

4 racks of lamb, each with 4 cutlets
2 tbsp extra-virgin olive oil
1 tbsp balsamic vinegar
1 tbsp lemon juice
3 tbsp finely chopped fresh rosemary
1 small onion, finely chopped
salt and pepper

sozzled lamb chops

SERVES	PREP	+5 mins	COOK
4	15 mins	marinating	10 mins

These chops will only need marinating for a short time, as the marinade is quite strongly flavoured.

1 Preheat the barbecue. Place the lamb chops in a large, shallow, non-metallic dish. Mix all the ingredients for the marinade together in a jug, seasoning to taste with salt and pepper. Pour the mixture over the chops and then turn them until they are thoroughly coated. Cover with clingfilm and leave to marinate for 5 minutes.

2 To make the mustard butter, mix all the ingredients together in a small bowl, beating with a fork until well blended. Cover with clingfilm and leave to chill in the refrigerator until required.

3 Drain the chops, reserving the marinade. Cook over medium hot coals, brushing frequently with the reserved marinade, for 5 minutes on each side. Transfer to serving plates, top with the mustard butter and garnish with parsley sprigs. Serve immediately with salad.

ingredients

8 lamb loin chops

marinade
2 tbsp extra-virgin olive oil
2 tbsp Worcestershire sauce
2 tbsp lemon juice
2 tbsp dry gin
1 garlic clove, finely chopped
salt and pepper

mustard butter
55 g/2 oz unsalted butter, softened
$1^1/2$ tsp tarragon mustard
1 tbsp chopped fresh parsley
dash of lemon juice

to garnish
fresh parsley sprigs

to serve
salad

lamb burgers with mint & pine kernels

SERVES
4

PREP
15
mins

+30
mins
chilling

COOK
5-10
mins

These tasty burgers have a Greek flavour. Serve them in the traditional warmed pitta breads or in soft baps with salad.

1 Place the lamb mince, chopped onion, pine kernels, fresh mint and salt and pepper to taste in a large bowl and mix together until thoroughly combined. Using your hands, divide the mixture into 4 and shape the portions into round burgers, pressing the mixture together well. Leave to chill in the refrigerator for 30 minutes.

2 Preheat the barbecue. Cook the burgers over hot coals for 4–5 minutes on each side, turning once, until the juices run clear.

3 Warm the pitta breads at the side of the barbecue or toast the baps. Crumble the feta cheese into small pieces and reserve until required.

4 Line the pitta bread or baps with the salad leaves. Sandwich the burgers between the pitta bread or baps and top with the crumbled feta cheese.

ingredients

450 g/1 lb fresh lean lamb
  mince
1 small onion, finely chopped
50 g/1³/₄ oz pine kernels
2 tbsp chopped fresh mint
salt and pepper

to serve
4 pitta breads or soft baps
75 g/2³/₄ oz feta cheese
salad leaves

sweet lamb fillet

SERVES	PREP	COOK
4	5 mins	1 hr

Lamb fillet, enhanced by a sweet and spicy glaze, is cooked on the barbecue in a kitchen foil parcel for deliciously moist results.

1 Place the lamb fillet on a large piece of double thickness kitchen foil. Season with salt and pepper to taste.

2 Heat the oil in a small pan and fry the onion and garlic for 2–3 minutes until softened but not browned. Stir in the grated ginger and cook for 1 minute, stirring occasionally.

3 Stir in the apple juice, apple sauce, sugar, ketchup and mustard and bring to the boil. Boil rapidly for about 10 minutes until reduced by half. Stir the mixture occasionally so that it does not burn and stick to the base of the pan.

4 Brush half of the sauce over the lamb, then wrap up the lamb in the kitchen foil to completely enclose it. Barbecue the lamb parcels over hot coals for about 25 minutes, turning the parcel over occasionally.

5 Open out the kitchen foil and brush the lamb with some of the sauce. Continue to barbecue for a further 15–20 minutes or until cooked through.

6 Place the lamb on a chopping board, remove the foil and cut into thick slices. Transfer to serving plates and spoon over the remaining sauce. Serve with green salad leaves, croûtons and fresh crusty bread.

ingredients

2 fillets of neck of lean lamb, each
  225 g/8 oz
1 tbsp olive oil
$^1/_2$ onion, chopped finely
1 clove garlic, crushed
2.5 cm/1 inch piece root ginger,
  grated
5 tbsp apple juice
3 tbsp smooth apple sauce
1 tbsp light muscovado sugar
1 tbsp tomato ketchup
$^1/_2$ tsp mild mustard
salt and pepper

to serve
green salad leaves, croûtons and
  fresh crusty bread

ingredients

marinade
2 tsp vegetable oil
1 tsp curry powder
1 tsp garam masala
2 tsp granulated sugar
200 ml/7fl oz natural yogurt

skewers
400 g/14 oz boneless lamb, cubed
140 g/5 oz dried apricot halves
1 red or green pepper, deseeded
  and cut into small chunks
2 courgettes, cubed
16 baby onions

to garnish
fresh coriander leaves

to serve
freshly steamed or boiled rice
crisp green salad leaves

curried lamb skewers

SERVES	PREP		COOK
4	10 mins	**+8hrs** marinating	15-20 mins

A subtle combination of flavours makes this a stylish dish for a barbecue.

1 Put the oil, spices, sugar and yogurt into a large bowl and mix until well combined.

2 Thread the lamb onto 8 skewers, alternating it with the apricot halves, red pepper, courgettes and baby onions. When the skewers are full (leave a small space at either end), transfer them to the bowl and turn them in the yogurt mixture until they are well coated. Cover with clingfilm and place in the refrigerator to marinate for at least 8 hours or overnight.

3 When the skewers are thoroughly marinated, lift them out and barbecue them over hot coals, turning them frequently, for 15 minutes, or until the meat is cooked right through. Serve at once with freshly cooked rice or a crisp green salad, garnished with fresh coriander leaves.

lamb and wild mushroom brochettes

SERVES	PREP		COOK
6	**15** mins	**+4hrs** marinating	**15-20** mins

The earthy flavour of wild mushrooms goes well with the sweetness of the lamb.

1 Pour the wine, olive oil and lemon juice into a large, shallow dish and season with salt and pepper. Stir in the onion, garlic and thyme, then add the lamb and stir again to coat. Cover with clingfilm and marinate in the refrigerator for 4 hours.

2 Drain the lamb, reserving the marinade. Loosely roll up the bacon rashers. Thread the cubes of lamb, bacon rolls and mushrooms alternately onto 6 long skewers and finish each with a cherry tomato.

3 Brush the brochettes generously with the reserved marinade. Grill on a medium barbecue, turning and brushing occasionally with the marinade, for about 15 minutes, or until cooked through and tender. Garnish with fresh rosemary and serve immediately, with a rice salad.

ingredients

125 ml/4 fl oz red wine
6 tbsp olive oil
1 tbsp lemon juice
salt and pepper
1 large onion, chopped
2 garlic cloves, finely chopped
1 tbsp chopped fresh thyme
1 kg/2 lb 4 oz boned leg
 of lamb, cut into 2.5-cm/
 1-inch cubes
12 rashers streaky bacon,
 rinds removed
24 wild mushrooms
6 cherry tomatoes

to garnish
rosemary sprig

to serve
rice salad

spicy lamb steaks

SERVES	PREP	+3hrs	COOK
4	15 mins	20mins cooling/ marinating	40 mins

Lamb, fresh rosemary and bay leaves always go so well together, and here a hot and spicy marinade is used to perfection.

1 To make the marinade, heat the oil in a heavy-based saucepan. Add the onion and garlic and cook, stirring occasionally, for 5 minutes, or until softened. Stir in the jerk seasoning, curry paste and grated ginger and cook, stirring constantly, for 2 minutes. Add the tomatoes, Worcestershire sauce and sugar, then season to taste with salt and pepper. Bring to the boil, stirring constantly, then reduce the heat and simmer for 15 minutes, or until thickened. Remove from the heat and leave to cool.

2 Place the lamb steaks between 2 sheets of clingfilm and beat with the side of a rolling pin to flatten. Transfer the steaks to a large, shallow, non-metallic dish. Pour the marinade over them, turning to coat. Cover with clingfilm and leave to marinate in the refrigerator for 3 hours.

3 Preheat the barbecue. Drain the lamb, reserving the marinade. Cook the lamb over medium hot coals, brushing frequently with the marinade, for 5–7 minutes on each side. Meanwhile, dip the rosemary and bay leaves in the olive oil and cook on the barbecue for 3–5 minutes. Serve the lamb immediately with the herbs.

ingredients

4 lamb steaks, about 175 g/
  6 oz each
8 fresh rosemary sprigs
8 fresh bay leaves
2 tbsp olive oil

spicy marinade

2 tbsp sunflower oil
1 large onion, finely chopped
2 garlic cloves, finely chopped
2 tbsp jerk seasoning
1 tbsp curry paste
1 tsp grated fresh root ginger
400 g/14 oz canned chopped
  tomatoes
4 tbsp Worcestershire sauce
3 tbsp light muscovado sugar
salt and pepper

turkish kebabs

SERVES	PREP		COOK
4	20 mins	+2hrs marinating	10-15 mins

Turkey has an eclectic mix of influences in its cooking style. These traditional kebabs would originally have been made with mutton or goat.

1 Place the lamb cubes in a large, shallow, non-metallic dish. Mix the olive oil, wine, mint, garlic, orange rind, paprika and sugar together in a jug and season to taste with salt and pepper. Pour the mixture over the lamb, turning to coat, then cover with clingfilm and leave to marinate in the refrigerator for 2 hours, turning occasionally.

2 Preheat the barbecue. To make the tahini cream, put the tahini paste, garlic, oil and lemon juice into a food processor and process briefly to mix. With the motor still running, gradually add the water through the feeder tube until smooth. Transfer to a bowl, cover with clingfilm and leave to chill in the refrigerator until required.

3 Drain the lamb, reserving the marinade, and thread it on to several long metal skewers. Cook over medium hot coals, turning and brushing frequently with the reserved marinade, for 10–15 minutes. Serve with the tahini cream.

ingredients

500 g/1 lb 2 oz boned shoulder
  of lamb, cut into 2.5-cm/
  1-inch cubes
1 tbsp olive oil
2 tbsp dry white wine
2 tbsp finely chopped
  fresh mint
4 garlic cloves, finely chopped
2 tsp grated orange rind
1 tbsp paprika
1 tsp sugar
salt and pepper

tahini cream
225 g/8 oz tahini paste
2 garlic cloves, finely chopped
2 tbsp extra-virgin olive oil
2 tbsp lemon juice
125 ml/4 fl oz water

butterfly lamb with balsamic vinegar & mint

SERVES	PREP		COOK
4	20 mins	**+6hrs** marinating	1 hrs

The appearance of the leg of lamb as it is opened out to cook on the barbecue gives this dish its name.

1 Open out the boned leg of lamb so that its shape resembles a butterfly. Thread 2–3 skewers through the meat to make it easier to turn on the barbecue.

2 Mix the balsamic vinegar, lemon rind and juice, sunflower oil, mint, garlic, sugar and salt and pepper to taste together in a non-metallic dish that is large enough to hold the lamb. Place the lamb in the dish and turn it over a few times so that the meat is coated on both sides with the marinade. Cover and leave to marinate in the refrigerator for at least 6 hours, or preferably overnight, turning occasionally.

3 Preheat the barbecue. Remove the lamb from the marinade and reserve the liquid for basting. Place the rack about 15 cm/6 inches above the coals and cook the lamb for 30 minutes on each side, turning once and basting frequently with the marinade.

4 Transfer the lamb to a chopping board and remove the skewers. Cut the lamb into slices across the grain and serve with grilled vegetables and salad leaves.

ingredients

boned leg of lamb, about
  1.8 kg/4 lb
8 tbsp balsamic vinegar
grated rind and juice of 1 lemon
150 ml/5 fl oz sunflower oil
4 tbsp chopped fresh mint
2 garlic cloves, crushed
2 tbsp light muscovado sugar
salt and pepper

to serve
grilled vegetables
green salad leaves

lamb and feta cheese burgers

SERVES	PREP		COOK
4-6	10 mins	+30 mins chilling	8 mins

This combination of feta cheese, prunes, pine kernels and rosemary may sound rather unusual, but tastes fabulous.

1 Place the lamb mince in a large bowl with the cheese, garlic, spring onions, prunes, pine kernels and breadcrumbs. Mix well, breaking up any lumps of mince.

2 Add the rosemary and salt and pepper to the lamb mixture in the bowl. Mix together, then shape into 4–6 equal-sized burgers. Cover and leave to chill for 30 minutes.

3 Preheat the barbecue. Place the burgers on a grill rack and brush lightly with oil. Cook over medium hot coals for 4 minutes before turning over and brushing with the remaining oil. Continue to cook for 4 minutes, or until cooked to personal preference. Serve.

ingredients

450 g/1 lb fresh lamb mince
225 g/8 oz feta cheese, crumbled
2 garlic cloves, crushed
6 spring onions, finely chopped
85 g/3 oz ready-to-eat prunes, chopped
25 g/1 oz pine kernels, toasted
55 g/2 oz fresh wholemeal breadcrumbs
1 tbsp chopped fresh rosemary
salt and pepper
1 tbsp sunflower oil

persian lamb

SERVES
4-6

PREP
15
mins

+2-3
hrs
marinating

COOK
25
mins

Chargrilling and lamb seem to be made for each other, and all over the Middle East both lamb and mutton are enjoyed in this way.

1 For the marinade, combine the mint, yogurt, garlic and pepper.

2 Put the chops into a non-porous dish and rub all over with the lemon juice. Pour the marinade over the chops. Cover and marinate for 2–3 hours.

3 To make the tabbouleh. Put the couscous into a heatproof bowl and pour over the boiling water. Leave for 5 minutes. Drain and put into a sieve. Steam over a pan of barely simmering water for 8 minutes. Toss in the oil and lemon juice. Add the onion, tomato and herbs. Season and set aside.

4 Cook the lamb over a medium barbecue for 15 minutes, turning once. Serve with the tabbouleh.

ingredients

2 tbsp chopped fresh mint
225 ml/8 fl oz low-fat natural
  yogurt
4 garlic cloves, crushed
$1/4$ tsp pepper
6 lean lamb chops
2 tbsp lemon juice

tabbouleh
250 g/9 oz couscous
500 ml/18 fl oz boiling water
2 tbsp olive oil
2 tbsp lemon juice
$1/2$ onion, chopped finely
4 tomatoes, chopped
25 g/1 oz fresh coriander,
  chopped
2 tbsp chopped fresh mint
salt and pepper

shashlik

SERVES	PREP		COOK
4	20 mins	+8hrs marinating	10–15 mins

Shashlik are a Georgian speciality from the fertile area between the Black Sea and the Caucasian Mountains in the Russian Federation.

1 Place the lamb and mushrooms in a large, shallow, non-metallic dish. Mix all the ingredients for the marinade together in a jug, seasoning to taste with salt and pepper. Pour the mixture over the lamb and mushrooms, turning to coat. Cover with clingfilm and leave to marinate in the refrigerator for up to 8 hours.

2 Preheat the barbecue. Cut the bacon rashers in half across the centre and stretch with a heavy, flat-bladed knife, then roll up. Drain the lamb and mushrooms, reserving the marinade. Thread the bacon rolls, lamb, mushrooms, tomatoes and green pepper squares alternately on to metal skewers. Sieve the marinade.

3 Cook the kebabs over medium hot coals, turning and brushing frequently with the reserved marinade, for 10–15 minutes. Transfer to a large serving plate, garnish with fresh herb sprigs and serve immediately.

ingredients

675 g/1 lb 8 oz boneless
 leg of lamb, cut into 2.5-cm/
 1-inch cubes
12 large mushrooms
4 streaky bacon rashers, rinded
8 cherry tomatoes
1 large green pepper, deseeded
 and cut into squares

marinade
4 tbsp sunflower oil
4 tbsp lemon juice
1 onion, finely chopped
$1/2$ tsp dried rosemary
$1/2$ tsp dried thyme
salt and pepper

to garnish
fresh herb sprigs

chickenwingsspicymarinadeyumyumjuicy
duckdrumsticks...

poultry

mustard & honey drumsticks

SERVES	PREP		COOK
4	**10** mins	**+1hr** marinating	**25–30** mins

Chicken can taste rather bland, but this sweet-and-sour glaze gives it a wonderful piquancy and helps to keep it moist during cooking.

1 Using a sharp knife, make 2–3 diagonal slashes in the chicken drumsticks and place them in a large, non-metallic dish.

2 Mix all the ingredients for the glaze together in a jug and season to taste with salt and pepper. Pour the glaze over the drumsticks, turning until the drumsticks are well coated. Cover with clingfilm and leave to marinate in the refrigerator for at least 1 hour.

3 Preheat the barbecue. Drain the chicken drumsticks, reserving the marinade. Cook the chicken over medium hot coals, turning frequently and brushing with the reserved marinade, for 25–30 minutes, or until thoroughly cooked. Transfer to serving plates, garnish with fresh parsley sprigs and serve immediately with salad.

ingredients

8 chicken drumsticks

glaze
125 ml/4 fl oz clear honey
4 tbsp Dijon mustard
4 tbsp wholegrain mustard
4 tbsp white wine vinegar
2 tbsp sunflower oil
salt and pepper

to garnish
fresh parsley sprigs

to serve
salad

the ultimate chicken burger

SERVES **4**

PREP **10** mins

+30 mins chilling

COOK **15-20** mins

ingredients

4 large chicken breast fillets, skinned
1 large egg white
1 tbsp cornflour
1 tbsp plain flour
1 egg, beaten
55 g/2 oz fresh white breadcrumbs
2 tbsp sunflower oil
2 beef tomatoes, sliced

These deliciously tender, thin pieces of breaded chicken, served with ketchup or mayonnaise, will go down well with all the chicken enthusiasts you know.

1 Place the chicken breasts between 2 sheets of non-stick baking paper and flatten slightly using a meat mallet or a rolling pin. Beat the egg white and cornflour together, then brush over the chicken. Cover and leave to chill for 30 minutes, then coat in the flour.

2 Place the egg and breadcrumbs in 2 separate bowls and coat the burgers first in the egg, allowing any excess to drip back into the bowl, then in the breadcrumbs.

3 Preheat the barbecue. Lightly brush each burger with a little oil and then add them to the barbecue grill, cooking over medium hot coals for 6-8 minutes on each side, or until thoroughly cooked. If you are in doubt, it is worth cutting one of the burgers in half. If there is any sign of pinkness, cook for a little longer to get that nice barbecue taste. Add the tomato slices to the grill rack for the last 1–2 minutes of the cooking time to heat through. Serve.

zesty kebabs

SERVES **4**

PREP **10** **mins**

+8hrs marinating

COOK **6-10** mins

These lovely, fresh-tasting chicken kebabs are marinated in a zingy mixture of citrus juice and rind.

1 Using a sharp knife, cut the chicken into 2.5-cm/1-inch cubes, then place them in a large glass bowl. Place the lemon and orange rind, the lemon and orange juice, the honey, oil, mint and ground coriander in a jug and mix together. Season to taste with salt and pepper. Pour the marinade over the chicken cubes and toss until they are thoroughly coated. Cover with clingfilm and leave to marinate in the refrigerator for up to 8 hours.

2 Preheat the barbecue. Drain the chicken cubes, reserving the marinade. Thread the chicken on to several long metal skewers.

3 Cook the skewers over medium hot coals, turning and brushing frequently with the reserved marinade, for 6–10 minutes, or until thoroughly cooked. Transfer to a large serving plate, garnish with fresh mint sprigs and citrus zest and serve immediately.

ingredients

4 skinless, boneless chicken breasts, about 175 g/6 oz each
finely grated rind and juice of $1/2$ lemon
finely grated rind and juice of $1/2$ orange
2 tbsp clear honey
2 tbsp olive oil
2 tbsp chopped fresh mint
$1/4$ tsp ground coriander
salt and pepper

to garnish
fresh mint sprigs
citrus zest

pesto and ricotta chicken with tomato vinaigrette

SERVES	PREP	+30 mins chilling	COOK
4	15 mins		20 mins

The flavours and aromas of the Mediterranean turn a simple piece of chicken into a summer feast.

1 Mix together the pesto and ricotta in a small bowl until well combined. Using a sharp knife, cut a deep slit in the side of each chicken breast to make a pocket. Spoon the ricotta mixture into the pockets and re-shape the chicken breasts to enclose it. Place the chicken on a plate, cover and chill for 30 minutes.

2 To make the vinaigrette, pour the olive oil into a blender or food processor, add the chives and process until smooth. Scrape the mixture into a bowl and stir in the tomatoes, lime juice and rind. Season to taste with salt and pepper.

3 Brush the chicken with the olive oil and season with pepper. Grill on a fairly hot barbecue for about 8 minutes on each side, or until cooked through and tender. Transfer to serving plates, spoon over the vinaigrette and serve immediately.

ingredients

1 tbsp pesto sauce
115 g/4 oz ricotta cheese
4 x 175 g/6 oz skinless, boneless
  chicken breasts
1 tbsp olive oil
ground black pepper

to garnish
small salad

tomato vinaigrette
100 ml/3$^{1}/_{2}$ fl oz olive oil
1 bunch fresh chives
500 g/1 lb 2 oz tomatoes, peeled,
  deseeded and chopped
juice and finely grated rind of
  1 lime
salt and ground black pepper

ingredients

4 duck breasts, about 225 g/
  8 oz each
4 tbsp maple syrup
juice and finely grated rind
  of 1 orange
juice and finely grated rind
  of 1 lemon

cranberry relish

225 g/8 oz fresh or frozen
  cranberries
2 shallots, finely chopped
150 ml/5 fl oz red wine
115 g/4 oz caster sugar
2 tsp cornflour
juice and finely grated rind
  of 1 orange
1 tsp ground allspice

duck breasts with maple syrup and cranberry relish

SERVES
4

PREP
10
mins

+30
mins
chilling

COOK
35
mins

The slight sharpness of the relish contrasts delightfully with the sweet glaze and rich meat.

1 For the relish, put the cranberries, shallots, wine and sugar into a saucepan and bring to the boil, stirring. Reduce the heat and simmer for 10–15 minutes, until soft. Mix together the cornflour, orange juice and allspice in a small bowl, then stir into the cranberries. Add the orange rind and cook, stirring, until thickened. Remove from the heat, cover and cool, then chill until ready to serve.

2 Cut off any excess fat from the duck breasts and score the skin. Cut the duck breasts into 2.5-cm/1-inch cubes and thread onto skewers. Mix together the maple syrup, orange juice and rind and lemon juice and rind in a bowl.

3 Barbecue the duck breasts for 2 minutes on each side, then brush with the maple syrup mixture. Grill, turn and brush with the maple syrup mixture frequently, for about 8 minutes, or until cooked through and tender. Serve immediately, with the cranberry relish.

jerk chicken

SERVES
4

PREP
15
mins

+24hrs
marinating

COOK
30
mins

This is perhaps one of the best known Caribbean dishes. The 'jerk' in the name refers to the hot spicy coating.

ingredients

4 lean chicken portions
1 bunch spring onions, trimmed
1–2 Scotch Bonnet chillies, deseeded
1 garlic clove
5 cm/2 inch piece root ginger, peeled and roughly chopped
1/2 tsp dried thyme
1/2 tsp paprika
1/4 tsp ground allspice
pinch ground cinnamon
pinch ground cloves
4 tbsp white wine vinegar
3 tbsp light soy sauce
pepper

1 Rinse the chicken portions and pat them dry on absorbent kitchen paper. Place them in a shallow dish.

2 Place the spring onions, chillies, garlic, ginger, thyme, paprika, allspice, cinnamon, cloves, wine vinegar, soy sauce and pepper to taste in a food processor and process until smooth.

3 Pour the spicy mixture over the chicken. Turn the chicken portions over so that they are well coated in the marinade.

4 Transfer the chicken portions to the refrigerator and leave to marinate for up to 24 hours.

5 Remove the chicken from the marinade and barbecue over medium hot coals for about 30 minutes, turning the chicken over and basting occasionally with any remaining marinade, until the chicken is browned and cooked through.

6 Transfer the chicken portions to individual serving plates and serve at once.

chicken skewers with lemon & coriander

SERVES	PREP		COOK
4	**10** mins	**+2hrs** marinating	**15** mins

These tasty chicken kebabs are perfect served as part of a barbecue lunch party with a crisp salad and a delicious lemon yoghurt dressing.

1 Using a sharp knife, cut the chicken into 2.5-cm/1-inch pieces and place in a shallow, non-metallic dish.

2 Add the ground coriander, lemon juice, salt and pepper to taste and 4 tablespoons of the yogurt to the chicken and mix together with a wooden spoon until thoroughly combined. Cover with clingfilm and leave to chill in the refrigerator for at least 2 hours, preferably overnight.

3 Preheat the barbecue. To make the lemon yogurt, peel and finely chop the lemon, discarding any pips. Stir the lemon into the remaining yogurt together with the chopped coriander. Chill in the refrigerator until required.

4 Thread the chicken pieces on to several presoaked wooden skewers. Brush the rack with sunflower oil and cook the chicken over hot coals for 15 minutes, basting with the oil.

5 Transfer the chicken skewers to warmed serving plates and garnish with coriander sprigs and lemon wedges. Serve with a selection of salad leaves and the lemon yogurt.

ingredients

4 skinless, boneless chicken
  breasts
1 tsp ground coriander
2 tsp lemon juice
salt and pepper
300 ml/10 fl oz natural yogurt
1 lemon
2 tbsp chopped fresh coriander
sunflower oil, for brushing

to serve
salad leaves

to garnish
fresh coriander sprigs
lemon wedges

barbecued chicken legs

SERVES	PREP	COOK
4	**5** mins	**20** mins

ingredients

12 chicken drumsticks

spiced butter
175 g/6 oz butter
2 garlic cloves, crushed
1 tsp grated ginger root
2 tsp ground turmeric
4 tsp cayenne pepper
2 tbsp lime juice
3 tbsp mango chutney

to serve
crisp green seasonal salad
boiled rice

Just the thing to put on the barbecue – chicken legs, coated with a spicy, curry-like butter, then grilled until crispy and golden.

1 To make the Spiced Butter mixture, beat the butter with the garlic, ginger, turmeric, cayenne pepper, lime juice and chutney until well blended.

2 Using a sharp knife, slash each chicken leg to the bone 3-4 times.

3 Cook the drumsticks over a moderate barbecue for about 12-15 minutes or until almost cooked. Alternatively, grill the chicken for about 10-12 minutes until almost cooked, turning halfway through.

4 Spread the chicken legs liberally with the butter mixture and continue to cook for a further 5-6 minutes, turning and basting frequently with the butter until golden and crisp. Serve the chicken legs hot or cold with a crisp green salad and rice.

hot red chicken

SERVES **4**

PREP **10** **mins**

+8hrs marinating

COOK **25–30** **mins**

In this adaptation of a traditional Indian recipe for spring chickens, chicken pieces are used and are just as tasty.

1 Place the curry paste, tomato ketchup, five-spice powder, chilli, Worcestershire sauce and sugar in a small bowl, and stir until the sugar has dissolved. Season to taste with salt.

2 Place the chicken pieces in a large, shallow, non-metallic dish and spoon the spice paste over them, rubbing it in well. Cover with clingfilm and leave to marinate in the refrigerator for up to 8 hours.

3 Preheat the barbecue. Remove the chicken from the spice paste, discarding any remaining paste, and brush with oil. Cook the chicken over medium hot coals, turning occasionally, for 25–30 minutes. Briefly heat the naan bread on the barbecue and serve with the chicken, garnished with lemon wedges and coriander sprigs.

ingredients

1 tbsp curry paste
1 tbsp tomato ketchup
1 tsp Indian five-spice powder
1 fresh red chilli, deseeded and finely chopped
1 tsp Worcestershire sauce
1 tsp sugar
salt
8 skinless chicken pieces
vegetable oil, for brushing

to serve
naan bread

to garnish
lemon wedges
fresh coriander sprigs

maple-glazed turkey burgers

SERVES	PREP		COOK
4	**15** mins	**+1hr** chilling	**16-19** mins

ingredients

2 corn on the cobs with leaves
  intact
450 g/1 lb fresh turkey mince
1 red pepper, deseeded, peeled
  and finely chopped
6 spring onions, finely chopped
55 g/2 oz fresh white
  breadcrumbs
2 tbsp chopped fresh basil
salt and pepper
1 tbsp sunflower oil
2 tbsp maple syrup

To give the meal and authentic taste of the American deep south, serve with corn fritters and fried bananas tossing in lemon juice.

1 Preheat the barbecue. Cook the corn on the cobs over hot coals for 8-10 minutes, turning every 2–3 minutes, or until the leaves are charred. Remove from the grill rack, leave to cool, then strip off the leaves and silky threads. Using a sharp knife, cut away the kernels and place in a bowl.

2 Add the turkey mince, red pepper, spring onions, breadcrumbs, basil, salt and pepper to the sweetcorn kernels in the bowl. Mix together, then shape into 4 equal-sized burgers. Cover and leave to chill for 1 hour.

3 Move the grill rack up to reduce the heat, brush grill and burgers very lightly with a little oil. The brush 1 teaspoon of maple syrup over each burger and cook over medium hot coals for 4 minutes. Turn the burgers over and cook for a further 4–5 minutes, or until the burgers are cooked through. Pour over the remaining maple syrup and serve.

drumsticks in a piquant dressing

SERVES	PREP	+20	COOK
6	10 mins	mins cooling	2 hrs

This tasty dressing gives the chicken drumsticks a rich colour as well as a fabulous flavour, which makes them irresistibly appetizing.

1 Preheat the barbecue. To make the dressing, place all the ingredients in a heavy-based saucepan and bring to the boil over a low heat. Cover and simmer gently for 1 hour, or until the onion and celery are very tender. Remove the saucepan from the heat and leave to cool.

2 Transfer the dressing to a food processor and process to a purée. Using a metal spoon, gently rub the purée through a fine-meshed sieve into a clean saucepan and bring to the boil over a low heat. Simmer gently for 25 minutes, or until reduced and thickened.

3 Brush the drumsticks with the sauce and cook over medium hot coals, turning and brushing with the sauce frequently, for 25–30 minutes. Serve. If you wish to serve the remaining sauce with the drumsticks, make sure that it is returned to boiling point first.

ingredients

12 chicken drumsticks

dressing
1 onion, chopped
1 celery stick, chopped
1 garlic clove, finely chopped
800 g/1 lb 12 oz canned
  chopped tomatoes
3 tbsp muscovado sugar
1 tbsp paprika
¼ tsp Tabasco sauce
1 tbsp Worcestershire sauce
pepper

ingredients

3 skinless, boneless chicken breasts
6 tbsp olive oil
4 tbsp lemon juice
$\frac{1}{2}$ small onion, grated
1 tbsp chopped fresh sage
8 tbsp sage and onion stuffing mix
6 tbsp boiling water
2 green peppers, deseeded
sunflower oil, for oiling

sauce
1 tbsp olive oil
1 red pepper, deseeded and
  finely chopped
1 small onion, finely chopped
pinch of sugar
210 g/7$\frac{1}{2}$ oz canned chopped
  tomatoes

chicken skewers with red pepper sauce

SERVES	PREP		COOK
4	**15** mins	**+1hr** marinating/ chilling	**35** mins

These kebabs are rather special and are well worth the extra effort needed to prepare them.

1 Cut the chicken into even-sized pieces. Mix the olive oil, lemon juice, grated onion and sage together and pour the mixture into a polythene bag. Add the chicken, seal the bag and shake to coat the chicken. Leave to marinate for at least 30 minutes, shaking the bag occasionally.

2 Place the stuffing mix in a small bowl and add the boiling water, stirring to mix well. Using a sharp knife, cut each pepper into 6 strips, then blanch them in boiling water for 3–4 minutes, or until softened. Drain and refresh under cold running water, then drain again.

3 Form 1 teaspoon of the stuffing mixture into a ball and roll it up in a strip of pepper. Repeat for the remaining stuffing mixture and pepper strips. Thread the pepper rolls on to several metal skewers alternately with pieces of chicken. Leave to chill in the refrigerator until required.

4 Preheat the barbecue. To make the sauce, heat the olive oil in a small saucepan. Add the red pepper and onion and fry for 5 minutes. Add the sugar and tomatoes and simmer for 5 minutes. Keep warm.

5 Cook the skewers on an oiled rack over hot coals, basting frequently with the remaining marinade, for 15 minutes, or until the chicken is cooked. Serve with the red pepper sauce.

115

sesame chicken brochettes with cranberry sauce

MAKES
8

PREP
15
mins

+30
mins
chilling

COOK
20-22
mins

The cranberries give the sauce a lovely tart flavour. It can be served hot or cold.

1 Cut the chicken into 2.5 cm/1 inch pieces. Put the wine, sugar, oil and salt and pepper to taste in a large bowl, stirring to combine. Add the chicken pieces and toss to coat. Leave to marinate for at least 30 minutes, turning the chicken occasionally.

2 To make the sauce, place the ingredients in a small saucepan and bring slowly to the boil, stirring. Simmer gently for 5–10 minutes until the cranberries are soft and pulpy. Taste and add a little extra sugar if wished. Keep warm or leave to chill as required.

3 Remove the chicken pieces from the marinade with a perforated spoon. Thread the chicken pieces on to 8 skewers, spacing them slightly apart to ensure even cooking.

4 Barbecue on an oiled rack over hot coals for 4–5 minutes on each side until just cooked. Brush several times with the marinade during cooking.

5 Remove the chicken skewers from the rack and roll in the sesame seeds. Return to the barbecue and cook for about 1 minute on each side or until the sesame seeds are toasted. Serve with the cranberry sauce, new potatoes and green salad leaves.

ingredients

4 chicken breasts, skinned and
  boned
4 tbsp dry white wine
1 tbsp light muscovado sugar
2 tbsp sunflower oil
100 g/$3^{1}/_{2}$ oz sesame seeds
salt and pepper

to serve
boiled new potatoes
green salad leaves

sauce
175 g/6 oz cranberries
150 ml/5 fl oz/$^{2}/_{3}$ cup
  cranberry juice drink
2 tbsp light muscovado sugar

117

spicy chicken wings

SERVES	PREP		COOK
4	**15** mins	**+8hrs** marinating	**18-20** mins

ingredients

16 chicken wings
4 tbsp sunflower oil
4 tbsp light soy sauce
5-cm/2-inch piece fresh root
  ginger, roughly chopped
2 garlic cloves, roughly chopped
juice and grated rind of 1 lemon
2 tsp ground cinnamon
2 tsp ground turmeric
4 tbsp clear honey
salt and pepper

sauce
2 orange peppers
2 yellow peppers
sunflower oil, for brushing
125 ml/4 fl oz natural yogurt
2 tbsp dark soy sauce
2 tbsp chopped fresh coriander

These delicious chicken wings are coated in a spicy marinade and served with a colourful, chargrilled pepper sauce.

1 Place the chicken wings in a large, shallow, non-metallic dish. Put the oil, soy sauce, ginger, garlic, lemon rind and juice, cinnamon, turmeric and honey into a food processor and process to a smooth purée. Season to taste with salt and pepper. Spoon the mixture over the chicken wings and turn until thoroughly coated, cover with clingfilm and leave to marinate in the refrigerator for up to 8 hours.

2 Preheat the barbecue. To make the sauce, brush the peppers with the oil and cook over hot coals, turning frequently, for 10 minutes, or until the skin is blackened and charred. Remove from the barbecue and leave to cool slightly, then peel off the skins and discard the seeds. Put the flesh into a food processor with the yogurt and process to a smooth purée. Transfer to a bowl and stir in the soy sauce and chopped coriander.

3 Drain the chicken wings, reserving the marinade. Cook over medium hot coals, turning and brushing frequently with the reserved marinade, for 8-10 minutes, or until thoroughly cooked. Serve immediately with the sauce.

duck breasts with caesar salad

SERVES	PREP.		COOK
6	15 mins	+12hrs marinating	15 mins

This is a marriage made in heaven – the richness of the duck is complemented by the refreshing salad.

1 Put the coriander seeds, juniper berries, peppercorns and bay leaves into a mortar and add ½ tsp salt. Grind to a powder. Rub the duck breasts all over with the spice mixture. Place on a dish, cover and marinate in the refrigerator overnight.

2 An hour before you are ready to cook, remove the duck from the refrigerator and wipe off most of the spice mix with kitchen paper. Whisk together the orange juice and olive oil in a small bowl and set aside.

3 Meanwhile, prepare the salad. Put the anchovies, lemon juice, garlic, mustard and egg yolk in a blender or food processor and process until smooth. With the machine running, gradually trickle in the olive oil until the dressing emulsifies. Season to taste. Place the lettuce in a bowl, add half the dressing and 3 tbsp of the Parmesan. Toss well.

4 Preheat the barbecue. Brush the duck breasts with the orange juice mixture and grill over hot coals, skin-side down, for 5 minutes. Turn, brush with more juice mixture and grill for 10–12 minutes, or until cooked to your liking. Leave to rest for 2–3 minutes, then slice into strips.

5 Divide the lettuce among 6 plates, sprinkle with the bread cubes and top with the duck. Drizzle over the remaining dressing, sprinkle with the remaining Parmesan and serve.

ingredients

1 tbsp coriander seeds
10 juniper berries
1 tsp green peppercorns
6 dried bay leaves, crumbled
500 g/1 lb 2 oz boneless duck breasts
1 tbsp orange juice
1 tbsp olive oil
salt and pepper

caesar salad
4 canned anchovy fillets, chopped
6 tbsp lemon juice
2 garlic cloves, chopped
2 tsp Dijon mustard
1 large egg yolk
300 ml/10 fl oz olive oil
1 large cos lettuce, torn into pieces
4 tbsp freshly grated Parmesan cheese
4 slices of bread, cubed and fried
  until crisp

thai-style chicken chunks

SERVES	PREP	+2¹/₂	COOK
4	**10** mins	**hrs** marinating	**20** mins

ingredients

marinade
1 red chilli and 1 green chilli,
  deseeded and finely chopped
2 garlic cloves, chopped
50 g/1³/₄ oz chopped fresh coriander
1 tbsp finely chopped fresh lemon-grass
¹/₂ tsp ground turmeric
¹/₂ tsp garam masala
2 tsp brown sugar
2 tbsp fish sauce
1 tbsp lime juice
salt and pepper

chicken
4 skinless, boneless chicken
  breasts, cut into small chunks

to garnish
chopped fresh coriander

to serve
freshly cooked jasmine rice

Ensure that you marinade the chicken for at least 2¹/₂ hours to bring out the variety of fantastic flavours.

1 Put the red and green chillies, garlic, coriander and lemon grass into a food processor and process until roughly chopped. Add the turmeric, garam masala, sugar, fish sauce and lime juice, season with salt and pepper and blend until smooth.

2 Put the chicken chunks into a non-metallic (glass or ceramic) bowl, which will not react with acid. Pour over enough marinade to cover the chicken, then cover with clingfilm and refrigerate for at least 2¹/₂ hours. Cover the remaining marinade with clingfilm and refrigerate until the chicken is ready.

3 When the chicken chunks are thoroughly marinated, lift them out and barbecue them over hot coals for 20 minutes or until cooked right through, turning them frequently and basting with the remaining marinade. Arrange the chicken on serving plates with some freshly cooked jasmine rice. Garnish with chopped fresh coriander and serve.

prawnsfreshfishtunaburgertantalising
salmonseabass...

fish &
seafood

prawns with citrus salsa

SERVES	PREP	COOK
6	25 mins	6 mins

A fruity, herby salsa brings out the flavour of grilled prawns and can be prepared in advance of the barbecue.

1 Preheat the barbecue. To make the salsa, peel the orange and cut into segments. Reserve any juice. Put the orange segments, apple quarters, chillies, garlic, coriander and mint into a food processor and process until smooth. With the motor running, add the lime juice through the feeder tube. Transfer the salsa to a serving bowl and season to taste with salt and pepper. Cover with clingfilm and leave to chill in the refrigerator until required.

2 Using a sharp knife, remove and discard the heads from the prawns, then peel off the shells. Cut along the back of the prawns and remove the dark intestinal vein. Rinse the prawns under cold running water and pat dry with kitchen paper. Mix the chopped coriander, cayenne and corn oil together in a dish. Add the prawns and toss well to coat.

3 Cook the prawns over medium hot coals for 3 minutes on each side, or until they have changed colour. Transfer to a large serving plate, garnish with fresh coriander leaves and serve immediately with lime wedges and the salsa.

ingredients

36 large, raw tiger prawns
2 tbsp finely chopped fresh coriander
pinch of cayenne pepper
3–4 tbsp corn oil

to garnish
fresh coriander leaves

to serve
lime wedges

salsa
1 orange
1 tart eating apple, peeled, quartered and cored
2 fresh red chillies, deseeded and chopped
1 garlic clove, chopped
8 fresh coriander sprigs
8 fresh mint sprigs
4 tbsp lime juice
salt and pepper

smoky trout burgers with pesto relish

SERVES	PREP		COOK
4	**10** mins	**+1hr** chilling	**25-30** mins

Smoked fish and bacon work really well together here, especially when teamed with the fresh and fragrant pesto relish.

ingredients

225 g/8 oz potatoes, cut into chunks
salt and pepper
350 g/12 oz smoked trout fillets, flaked
2 tsp creamed horseradish
6 spring onions, finely chopped
175 g/6 oz courgette, roughly grated
2 tbsp wholemeal flour
8 lean back bacon rashers
2 tbsp sunflower oil

pesto relish
15 g/^{1}/$_2$ oz fresh basil
40 g/1^1/$_2$ oz pine kernels, toasted
3 garlic cloves
150 ml/5 fl oz virgin olive oil
40 g/1^1/$_2$ oz Parmesan cheese, freshly grated
4-cm/1^1/$_2$-inch piece cucumber, peeled and finely diced
4 spring onions, finely chopped
2 plum tomatoes, finely diced

1 Cook the potatoes in a saucepan of lightly salted water for 15–20 minutes, or until cooked. Drain, mash and place in a large bowl. Add the trout, horseradish, spring onions, courgette and salt and pepper to taste. Mix together and shape into 4 equal-sized burgers. Leave to chill for 1 hour, then coat in the flour and wrap each in 2 rashers of bacon.

2 Meanwhile, prepare the relish. Place the basil, pine kernels and garlic in a food processor and blend for 1 minute. With the motor running, gradually pour in the oil and continue to blend until all the oil has been incorporated. Scrape into a bowl and stir in the cheese, cucumber, spring onions and tomatoes. Spoon into a serving bowl.

3 Preheat the barbecue. Lightly brush the burgers with oil and then cook over medium hot coals for 3-4 minutes on each side until golden and piping hot. Serve.

126

nut-crusted halibut

SERVES
4

PREP
5
mins

COOK
10
mins

This dish is sure to impress and is so easy you'll be amazed.

1 Brush the melted butter over the fish fillet.

2 Gently shake the fish to let any loose pistachios fall off.

3 Preheat the barbecue. Cook the halibut over medium coals for approximately 10 minutes, turning once. Cooking time will depend on the thickness of the fillet, but the fish should be firm and tender when done.

4 Remove the fish carefully from the rack to avoid the fish breaking up. Transfer to a large serving platter and serve immediately

ingredients

3 tbsp butter, melted
750 g/1 lb 10 oz halibut fillet
55 g/2 oz pistachio nuts,
  shelled and chopped very
  finely

barbecued trout

SERVES	PREP	COOK
4	15 mins	10 mins

Rainbow trout occasionally needs something extra to perk up its flavour. Try it cooked this way.

1 Rinse the trout inside and out under cold running water and thoroughly pat dry with kitchen paper.

2 Mix together the crushed chillies, paprika and salt in a small bowl. Sprinkle half this mixture inside the cavities of the fish and divide the chopped shallots among them.

3 Brush the outsides of the fish with oil, then sprinkle with a little more of the spices. Grill on a medium barbecue, brushing occasionally with more oil and sprinkling with the remaining spices, for 4–5 minutes on each side, or until the fish is cooked through and the flesh flakes easily. Serve immediately, garnished with lime wedges.

ingredients

4 rainbow trout, about 225–280 g/
   8–10 oz each, cleaned and heads
   removed
$^1/_2$ tsp crushed chillies
1 tbsp sweet paprika
1 tsp salt
4 small shallots, finely chopped
chilli oil, for brushing

to garnish
lime wedges

tasty thai fish patties

SERVES	PREP	+30	COOK
4	**10** mins	**mins** chilling	**5** mins

Bring the world of Thai food to your barbecue with these tasty patties. Serve with a good chilli or soy sauce.

1 Cut the fish into large pieces, place in a food processor with the onion and chilli (if using) and chop finely. Transfer the fish mixture to a mixing bowl and add all the other recipe ingredients. Mix well. The mixture should be quite thick and stiff. Preheat the barbecue.

2 Cover the bowl with clingfilm and refrigerate for at least 30 minutes. Remove the fish from the refrigerator and mix once more. Brush the grill rack with oil.

3 Form small patties from the fish mixture, place on a hot barbecue and cook in batches for 3–4 minutes, or until golden, turning once. If necessary, brush the rack with another tablespoon of oil before cooking the next batch of patties.

4 Transfer the cooked patties to a serving dish and garnish with coriander leaves and stalks of lemon grass. Serve warm or cold, accompanied by chilli sauce or sweet soy sauce.

ingredients

1 kg/2 lb 4 oz cod, haddock,
  whiting or coley fillet
  (skinned), or a mixture
1 small onion
1 small fresh chilli, deseeded
  (optional)
6–8 tbsp fresh breadcrumbs
1 egg
2 tbsp fish sauce
juice of $1/2$ lime
1 tbsp finely chopped fresh
  lemon-grass
2 tsp finely grated fresh ginger
2 tsp chopped fresh coriander
pinch of sugar
pinch of salt
1–2 tbsp vegetable oil, for brushing

to garnish
fresh coriander and lemon-grass

to serve
chilli sauce or sweet soy sauce

135

spanish prawns

SERVES	PREP	COOK
6	**20** mins	**25** mins

These fresh prawns are served with a fiery tomato and chilli sauce. For a milder flavour, reduce the number of chillies.

1 Preheat the barbecue. Chop enough parsley to fill 2 tablespoons and reserve. To make the sauce, deseed and chop the chillies, then put into a food processor with the onion and garlic and process until finely chopped. Add the tomatoes and olive oil and process to a purée.

2 Transfer the mixture to a saucepan set over a very low heat, stir in the sugar and season to taste with salt and pepper. Simmer very gently, without boiling, for 15 minutes. Transfer the sauce to an earthenware bowl and place on the side of the barbecue to keep warm.

3 Rinse the prawns under cold running water and pat dry on kitchen paper. Mix the parsley and olive oil in a dish, add the prawns and toss well to coat. Cook the prawns over medium hot coals for 3 minutes on each side, or until they have changed colour. Transfer to a plate, garnish with lemon wedges and serve with the sauce.

ingredients

1 bunch of fresh flat-leaf parsley
36 large, raw Mediterranean prawns,
  peeled and deveined, tails left on
3–4 tbsp olive oil

to garnish
lemon wedges

sauce
6 fresh red chillies
1 onion, chopped
2 garlic cloves, chopped
500 g/1 lb 2 oz tomatoes, chopped
3 tbsp olive oil
pinch of sugar
salt and pepper

ingredients

450 g/1 lb monkfish tail
2 courgettes
1 lemon
12 cherry tomatoes
8 bay leaves
4 tbsp olive oil
2 tbsp lemon juice
1 tsp chopped fresh thyme
$^1/_2$ tsp lemon pepper
salt

to serve
green salad leaves
fresh crusty bread

monkfish skewers with courgettes & lemon

SERVES	PREP	COOK
4	10 mins	20 mins

A simple basting sauce is brushed over these tasty kebabs, which make a perfect light meal served with bread and salad.

1 Preheat the barbecue. Using a sharp knife, cut the monkfish into 5-cm/2-inch chunks. Cut the courgettes into thick slices and the lemon into wedges.

2 Thread the monkfish, courgettes, lemon, tomatoes and bay leaves on to 4 metal skewers.

3 Mix the olive oil, lemon juice, thyme, lemon pepper and salt to taste together in a small bowl, then brush liberally all over the fish, lemon, tomatoes and bay leaves on the skewers.

4 Cook the skewers over medium hot coals for 15 minutes, basting frequently with the remaining oil mixture. Serve the skewers with green salad leaves and plenty of fresh crusty bread.

fresh tuna burgers with mango salsa

SERVES	PREP		COOK
4-6	15 mins	+1hr chilling	23-32 mins

Tuna is best eaten slightly pink as it can be rather dry if overcooked. It is also important that the burgers are piping hot before serving.

1 Cook the sweet potatoes in a saucepan of lightly salted boiling water for 15–20 minutes, or until tender. Drain well, then mash and place in a food processor. Cut the tuna into chunks and add to the potatoes.

2 Add the spring onions, courgette, chilli and mango chutney to the food processor and, using the pulse button, blend together. Shape into 4–6 equal-sized burgers, then cover and leave to chill for 1 hour.

3 Meanwhile make the salsa. Slice the mango flesh, reserving 8 good slices for serving. Finely chop the remainder, then mix with the tomatoes, chillies, cucumber, coriander and honey. Mix well, then spoon into a small bowl. Cover and leave for 30 minutes to allow the flavours to develop.

4 When the barbecue is hot, add the burgers and cook over medium hot coals for 4–6 minutes on each side or until piping hot. Serve.

ingredients

225 g/8 oz sweet potatoes, chopped
salt
450 g/1 lb fresh tuna steaks
6 spring onions, finely chopped
175 g/6 oz courgette, grated
1 fresh red jalapeño chilli, deseeded and finely chopped
2 tbsp prepared mango chutney
1 tbsp sunflower oil

mango salsa

1 large ripe mango, peeled and stoned
2 ripe tomatoes, finely chopped
4-cm/1$\frac{1}{2}$-inch piece cucumber, finely diced
1 fresh red jalapeño chilli, deseeded and finely chopped
1 tbsp chopped fresh coriander
1–2 tsp clear honey

fish burgers

SERVES	PREP		COOK
4	15 mins	+1hr chilling	23-30 mins

These burgers have a wonderful subtle smoky flavour due to the addition of smoked haddock.

1 Cook the potatoes in a saucepan of lightly salted boiling water for 15–20 minutes, or until tender. Drain well and mash. Chop the fish into small pieces, then place in a food processor with the mashed potatoes, lemon rind, parsley and salt and pepper to taste. Using the pulse button, blend together. Shape into 4 equal-sized burgers and coat in flour. Cover and leave to chill for 30 minutes.

2 Preheat the barbecue. Place the egg and breadcrumbs in 2 separate bowls and coat the burgers first in the egg, allowing any excess to drip back into the bowl, then in the breadcrumbs. Leave to chill for a further 30 minutes.

3 Lightly brush the burgers with oil. When the barbecue is hot, add the burgers and cook over medium hot coals for 4–5 minutes on each side or until golden and cooked through. Serve.

ingredients

140 g/5 oz potatoes, cut into chunks
salt and pepper
225 g/8 oz cod fillet, skinned
225 g/8 oz smoked haddock, skinned
1 tbsp grated lemon rind
1 tbsp chopped fresh parsley
1–2 tbsp plain flour
1 egg, beaten
85 g/3 oz fresh white breadcrumbs
2 tbsp sunflower oil

141

prawn & mixed pepper kebabs

SERVES	PREP	+3-4 hrs marinating	COOK
4	**15** mins		**4-5** mins

Zesty and with a bit of a kick, these kebabs are sure to jazz up your barbecue.

1 Put the spring onions, garlic, chillies, ginger, chives, lime juice, lime zest and chilli oil into a food processor and season well with salt and pepper. Process until smooth, then transfer to a non-metallic (glass or ceramic) bowl, which will not react with acid.

2 Thread the prawns onto skewers, alternating them with the red and green pepper chunks. When the skewers are full (leave a small space at either end), transfer them to the bowl and turn them in the mixture until they are well coated. Cover with clingfilm and place in the refrigerator to marinate for 3–4 hours.

3 Barbecue the kebabs over hot coals for 4–5 minutes or until the prawns are cooked right through (but do not overcook), turning them frequently and basting with the remaining marinade. Arrange the skewers on a bed of rice or Chinese leaves, garnish with lime wedges and serve.

ingredients

marinade
2 spring onions, trimmed and
    chopped
2 garlic cloves, finely chopped
1 green chilli and 1 small red chilli,
    deseeded and finely chopped
1 tbsp grated fresh root ginger
1 tbsp chopped fresh chives
4 tbsp lime juice
1 tbsp finely grated lime zest
2 tbsp chilli oil
salt and pepper

kebabs
24 large prawns, peeled and
    deveined, but with tails left on
1 red pepper and 1 green pepper,
    deseeded and cut into small chunks

to garnish
wedges of lime

to serve
freshly cooked rice or Chinese
    leaves

chargrilled tuna with chilli salsa

SERVES
4

PREP
15
mins

+1hr
marinating

COOK
20
mins

A firm fish such as tuna is an excellent choice for barbecues, as it is quite meaty and doesn't break up during cooking.

1 Rinse the tuna thoroughly under cold running water and pat dry with kitchen paper, then place in a large, shallow, non-metallic dish. Sprinkle the lime rind and juice and the olive oil over the fish. Season to taste with salt and pepper, cover with clingfilm and leave to marinate in the refrigerator for up to 1 hour.

2 Preheat the barbecue. To make the salsa, brush the peppers with the olive oil and cook over hot coals, turning frequently, for 10 minutes, or until the skin is blackened and charred. Remove from the barbecue and leave to cool slightly, then peel off the skins and discard the seeds. Put the peppers into a food processor with the remaining salsa ingredients and process to a purée. Transfer to a bowl and season to taste with salt and pepper.

3 Cook the tuna over hot coals for 4–5 minutes on each side, until golden. Transfer to serving plates, garnish with coriander sprigs and serve with the salsa.

ingredients

4 tuna steaks, about 175 g/
  6 oz each
grated rind and juice of 1 lime
2 tbsp olive oil
salt and pepper

to garnish
fresh coriander sprigs

chilli salsa
2 orange peppers
1 tbsp olive oil
juice of 1 lime
juice of 1 orange
2–3 fresh red chillies, deseeded
  and chopped
pinch of cayenne pepper

oriental prawn skewers

SERVES	PREP		COOK
4	**15** mins	**+2hrs** marinating	**4-5** mins

These prawn skewers are so easy and add a touch of the exotic to your barbecue platter.

1 Put the oils, lemon juice, rice wine, spring onions, garlic, ginger, lemon grass and coriander into a food processor and season well with salt and pepper. Process until smooth, then transfer to a non-metallic (glass or ceramic) bowl, which will not react with acid.

2 Add the prawns to the bowl and turn them in the mixture until they are well coated. Cover with clingfilm and place in the refrigerator to marinate for at least 2 hours.

3 When the prawns are thoroughly marinated, lift them out and thread them onto skewers leaving a small space at either end. Barbecue them with the lemon wedges over hot coals for 4–5 minutes or until cooked right through (but do not overcook), turning them frequently and basting with the remaining marinade. Arrange the skewers on a bed of freshly cooked jasmine rice, garnish with the lemon wedges and chopped fresh chives.

ingredients

marinade
100 ml/3^1/$_2$ fl oz vegetable oil
2 tbsp chilli oil
50 ml/2 fl oz lemon juice
1 tbsp rice wine or sherry
2 spring onions, trimmed and finely chopped
2 garlic cloves, finely chopped
1 tbsp grated fresh root ginger
1 tbsp chopped fresh lemon-grass
2 tbsp chopped fresh coriander
salt and pepper

skewers
1 kg/2 lb 4 oz large prawns, peeled and deveined, but with tails left on

to garnish
wedges of lemon
chopped fresh chives

to serve
freshly cooked jasmine rice

caribbean sea bass

SERVES	PREP	COOK
6	**15** mins	**20** mins

A fish basket is essential, as it is almost impossible to turn the fish without breaking it up and spoiling its appearance.

1 Preheat the barbecue. Rinse the sea bass inside and out under cold running water, then pat dry with kitchen paper. Using a sharp knife, make a series of shallow diagonal slashes along each side of the fish. Brush each slash with a little olive oil, then sprinkle over the saffron powder.

2 Brush a large fish basket with olive oil and place the fish in the basket, but do not close it. Season the cavity with salt and pepper. Place the lemon and lime slices and the thyme in the cavity without overfilling it.

3 Close the basket and cook the fish over medium hot coals for 10 minutes on each side. Carefully transfer to a large serving plate, garnish with lemon and lime slices and serve immediately.

ingredients

1.5 kg/3 lb 5 oz sea bass, cleaned
  and scaled
1–2 tsp olive oil
1 tsp saffron powder
salt and pepper
$^1/_2$ lemon, sliced, plus extra to
  garnish
1 lime, sliced, plus extra to garnish
1 bunch of fresh thyme

sea bream wrapped in vine leaves

ingredients

2 sea bream, about 350 g/12 oz
   each, cleaned and scaled

marinade
6 tbsp olive oil
2 tbsp white wine or dry sherry
2 garlic cloves, finely chopped
2 bay leaves, crumbled
1 tbsp fresh thyme leaves
1 tbsp snipped fresh chives
salt and pepper
12–16 large vine leaves

to garnish
thyme leaves
half a grilled lemon

SERVES	PREP		COOK
4	10-15 mins	**1hr** marinating **+20mins** soaking	15 mins

Vine leaves protect the delicate flesh of sea bream during cooking as well as imparting a subtle flavour.

1 Rinse the fish and pat dry with kitchen paper. Score both fish 2–3 times diagonally on each side and place in a large dish. Mix together the olive oil, white wine, garlic, bay leaves, thyme and chives in a small bowl and season with salt and pepper. Spoon the mixture over the fish, turning to coat. Cover and marinate for 1 hour.

2 If using vine leaves preserved in brine, soak them in hot water for 20 minutes, then rinse well and pat dry. If using fresh vine leaves, blanch in boiling water for 3 minutes, then refresh under cold water, drain and pat dry.

3 Drain the fish, reserving the marinade. Wrap each fish in vine leaves to enclose. Brush with the marinade. Grill on a medium barbecue for 6 minutes on each side, brushing with more marinade occasionally.

crunch!**vegetarianburger**mouthwatering
crispsalad**stuffed**tortillas...

vegetables

yam and red pepper burgers

SERVES
4-6

PREP
10
mins

+1hr
chilling

COOK
25-32
mins

**If you prefer a chunkier texture, blend the mixture only briefly
and do not peel the peppers.**

1 Cook the yam in a saucepan of lightly salted boiling water
for 15–20 minutes, or until tender. Drain well and place in
a food processor.

2 Add the chickpeas, red peppers, garlic, olives, sesame seeds,
coriander, and salt and pepper to the yam in the food
processor and, using the pulse button, blend together. Shape
into 4–6 equal-sized burgers, then coat in the flour. Cover and
leave to chill for 1 hour. Preheat the barbecue.

3 Lightly brush the burgers with oil. When the barbecue is
heated, add the burgers and cook over medium hot coals for
5–6 minutes on each side or until cooked and piping hot. Serve.

ingredients

225 g/8 oz yam, peeled and cut
  into chunks
salt and pepper
400 g/14 oz canned chickpeas,
  drained
2 red peppers, deseeded and
  peeled
2–3 garlic cloves, crushed
85 g/3 oz stoned black olives
2 tbsp sesame seeds
1 tbsp chopped fresh coriander
2 tbsp wholemeal flour
2 tbsp sunflower oil

corn-on-the-cob with blue cheese dressing

SERVES	PREP	COOK
6	**15** mins	**15-20** mins

Cook the corn cobs as soon after purchase as possible because they quickly lose their sweetness.

ingredients

140 g/5 oz Danish Blue cheese
140 g/5 oz curd cheese
125 ml/4 fl oz natural
  Greek yogurt
salt and pepper
6 corn cobs in their husks

1 Preheat the barbecue. Crumble the Danish Blue cheese, then place in a bowl. Beat with a wooden spoon until creamy. Beat in the curd cheese until thoroughly blended. Gradually beat in the yogurt and season to taste with salt and pepper. Cover with clingfilm and leave to chill in the refrigerator until required.

2 Fold back the husks on each corn cob and remove the silks. Smooth the husks back into place. Cut out 6 rectangles of foil, each large enough to enclose a corn cob. Wrap the corn cobs in the foil.

3 Cook the corn cobs over hot coals, turning frequently, for 15-20 minutes. Unwrap the corn cobs and discard the foil. Peel back the husk on one side of each and trim off with a sharp knife or kitchen scissors. Serve immediately with the blue cheese dressing.

spicy vegetarian sausages

SERVES	PREP	+45	COOK
4	**15** mins	**mins** chilling	**15** mins

Vegetarian sausages are no longer the poor relation with a recipe full of flavour and inspiration.

1 Put the garlic, onion, chilli, mashed kidney beans, breadcrumbs, almonds, rice and cheese into a large bowl. Stir in the egg yolk and oregano, then season with salt and plenty of pepper.

2 Using your hands, form the mixture into sausage shapes. Roll each sausage in a little flour, then transfer to a bowl, cover with clingfilm and refrigerate for 45 minutes.

3 Brush a piece of aluminium foil with oil, then put the sausages on the foil and brush them with a little more vegetable oil. Transfer the sausages and foil to the barbecue. Barbecue over hot coals, turning the sausages frequently, for about 15 minutes or until cooked right through. Serve with finger rolls, cooked sliced onion and tomato, and tomato ketchup and/or mustard.

ingredients

1 garlic clove, finely chopped
1 onion, finely chopped
1 red chilli, deseeded and
  finely chopped
400 g/14 oz canned red kidney
  beans, rinsed, drained and mashed
100 g/3^{1}/$_2$ oz fresh breadcrumbs
50 g/1^{3}/$_4$ oz almonds, toasted
  and ground
50 g/1^{3}/$_4$ oz cooked rice
50 g/1^{3}/$_4$ oz Cheddar cheese,
  grated
1 egg yolk
1 tbsp chopped fresh oregano
salt and pepper
flour, for dusting
vegetable oil, for brushing

to serve
fresh finger rolls
sliced onion, lightly cooked
sliced tomato, lightly cooked
tomato ketchup and/or mustard

marinated tofu skewers

SERVES	PREP		COOK
4	**20** mins	**+20 mins** marinating	**10-15** mins

Tofu is full of protein, vitamins and minerals, and it develops a fabulous flavour when it is marinated in garlic and herbs.

1 To make the marinade, mix the lemon rind and juice, garlic, rosemary, thyme and walnut oil together in a shallow dish. Drain the tofu, pat it dry on kitchen paper and cut it into squares. Add to the marinade and toss to coat. Leave to marinate for 20–30 minutes.

2 Preheat the barbecue. Deseed the peppers and cut into 2.5-cm/ 1-inch pieces. Blanch in boiling water for 4 minutes, refresh in cold water and drain. Using a canelle knife or potato peeler, remove strips of peel from the courgettes. Cut the courgettes into 2.5-cm/1-inch chunks.

3 Remove the tofu from the marinade, reserving the liquid for basting. Thread the tofu on to 8 presoaked wooden skewers, alternating with the peppers, courgette and button mushrooms.

4 Cook the skewers over medium hot coals for 6 minutes, turning and basting with the marinade. Transfer the skewers to warmed serving plates, garnish with carrot matchsticks and slices of lemon and serve.

ingredients

350 g/12 oz firm tofu
1 red pepper
1 yellow pepper
2 courgettes
8 button mushrooms

to garnish
carrot matchsticks
lemon slices

marinade
grated rind and juice of $1/2$ lemon
1 garlic clove, crushed
$1/2$ tsp chopped fresh rosemary
$1/2$ tsp chopped fresh thyme
1 tbsp walnut oil

ingredients

200 ml/7 fl oz natural Greek yogurt
$^1/_2$ cucumber
4 spring onions, finely chopped
1 garlic clove, finely chopped
3 tbsp chopped fresh mint
salt and pepper
2 tbsp olive oil
2 aubergines, thinly sliced

aubergines with tsatziki

SERVES	PREP	COOK
4	15 mins	10 mins

This makes a delicious appetizer for a barbecue party or can be served as part of a vegetarian barbecue meze.

1 First, make the tsatziki. Dice the cucumber. Place the yogurt in a bowl and beat well until smooth. Stir in the cucumber, spring onions, garlic and mint. Season to taste with salt and pepper. Transfer to a serving bowl, cover with clingfilm and chill in the refrigerator until required.

2 Season the olive oil to taste with plenty of salt and pepper, then brush the aubergine slices generously with the seasoned oil.

3 Cook the aubergines on a hot barbecue for 5 minutes on each side, brushing with more oil, if necessary. Serve immediately with the tsatziki.

vegetarian brochettes

SERVES	PREP	COOK
4	20 mins	8-10 mins

ingredients

2 courgettes
1 yellow pepper, deseeded
  and quartered
225 g/8 oz firm tofu
  (drained weight)
4 cherry tomatoes
4 baby onions
8 button mushrooms

honey glaze
2 tbsp olive oil
1 tbsp Meaux mustard
1 tbsp clear honey
salt and pepper

The great thing about tofu is its ability to absorb other flavours, in this case a mustard and honey flavoured glaze.

1 Preheat the barbecue. Using a vegetable peeler, peel off strips of skin along the length of the courgettes to leave alternate yellow and green stripes, then cut each courgette into 8 thick slices. Cut each of the yellow pepper quarters in half. Cut the drained tofu into 2.5-cm/1-inch cubes.

2 Thread the pieces of pepper, courgette slices, tofu cubes, cherry tomatoes, baby onions and button mushrooms on to 4 metal skewers. To make the glaze, mix the olive oil, mustard and honey together in a jug and season to taste with salt and pepper.

3 Brush the brochettes with the honey glaze and cook over medium hot coals, turning and brushing frequently with the glaze, for 8–10 minutes. Serve.

stuffed tortillas

SERVES	PREP	COOK
4	10-15 mins	15-17 mins

Here is a barbecue dish with a difference. Delicious, unusual and best of all – vegetarian!

1 Cook the red peppers on the barbecue, skin side down, for about 5 minutes or until the skins are blackened and charred. Transfer them to a polythene bag, seal the bag and set to one side.

2 Barbecue the sausages over hot coals for 10–12 minutes or until cooked right through, turning occasionally. While the sausages are cooking, put the kidney beans, tomatoes, onion, garlic, lime juice and basil into a large bowl. Season with salt and pepper and mix until well combined.

3 Take the red pepper quarters from the polythene bag and remove the blackened skins. Chop the flesh into small pieces and add it to the kidney bean mixture. About one minute before the sausages are ready, warm the tortillas on the barbecue for a few seconds.

4 Remove the sausages from the barbecue and cut them into slices. Fill the tortillas with sausage slices, kidney bean salsa, shredded lettuce, tomato slices and soured cream. Serve at once.

ingredients

2 red peppers, deseeded and cut into quarters
4 vegetarian sausages
325 g/11^1/$_2$ oz canned red kidney beans, drained, rinsed, and drained again
4 large tomatoes, chopped
1 large onion, chopped
1 garlic clove, chopped
1 tbsp lime juice
1 tbsp chopped fresh basil
salt and pepper
4 large wheat or corn tortillas, or 8 small ones

to serve
shredded lettuce
slices of fresh tomato
soured cream

163

the ultimate vegetarian burger

SERVES 4-6

PREP 10-12 mins

+1hr chilling

COOK 30-32 mins

ingredients

85 g/3 oz brown rice
salt and pepper
400 g/14 oz canned flageolet beans, drained
115 g/4 oz unsalted cashew nuts
3 garlic cloves
1 red onion, cut into wedges
115 g/4 oz sweetcorn kernels
2 tbsp tomato purée
1 tbsp chopped fresh oregano
2 tbsp wholemeal flour
2 tbsp sunflower oil

You can, if you like, substitute the flageolet beans for black-eyed or red kidney beans.

1 Preheat the barbecue. Cook the rice in a saucepan of lightly salted boiling water for 20 minutes, or until tender. Drain and place in a food processor.

2 Add the beans, cashew nuts, garlic, onion, sweetcorn, tomato purée, oregano and salt and pepper to the rice in the food processor and, using the pulse button, blend together. Shape into 4–6 equal-sized burgers, then coat in the flour. Cover and leave to chill for 1 hour.

3 Lightly brush the burgers with oil. When the barbecue is hot cook the burgers over medium hot coals for 5-6 minutes on each side or until cooked and piping hot. Serve.

vegetable satay

SERVES
4

PREP
10
mins

+4hrs
marinating

COOK
15
mins

Colourful vegetable kebabs are delightful served with a slightly crunchy peanut sauce.

1 Put the courgette and aubergine chunks, corn cobs and mushrooms in a bowl. Mix together the oil and lime juice in a jug and pour over the vegetables. Stir well, cover and leave to marinate for 4 hours.

2 To make the satay sauce, pour the coconut milk into a small saucepan and stir in the peanut butter. Heat gently, stirring constantly, until smooth. Stir in the soy sauce, sugar and the pinch of chilli powder. Transfer to the side of the barbecue to keep warm.

3 Drain the vegetables, reserving the marinade, and thread them alternately onto 4 skewers. Grill on a medium barbecue, turning occasionally for about 10 minutes. Serve immediately, with the satay sauce.

ingredients

marinade
3 courgettes, cut into 2.5-cm/
  1-inch chunks
1 aubergine, cut into 2.5-cm/
  1-inch chunks
8 baby corn cobs
8 button mushrooms
3 tbsp groundnut oil
3 tbsp lime juice

satay sauce
175 ml/6 fl oz canned
  coconut milk
115 g/4 oz crunchy peanut butter
2 tsp dark soy sauce
1 tsp muscovado sugar
pinch chilli powder

vegetable platter

SERVES	PREP		COOK
4	**25** mins	**+1hr** marinating	**30** mins

This cornucopia of chargrilled vegetables makes a wonderful vegetarian barbecue or accompaniment.

ingredients

2 red onions
2 white onions
2 fennel bulbs
6 baby corn cobs
12 cherry tomatoes
4 tbsp olive oil
1 tbsp lemon juice
3 garlic cloves, finely chopped
2 tbsp chopped fresh marjoram
salt and pepper
1 green pepper
1 yellow pepper
1 orange pepper
1 red pepper
1 tbsp sunflower oil

to serve
mayonnaise

1 Using a sharp knife, cut the red and white onions in half and reserve until required. Blanch the fennel and corn cobs in a large saucepan of boiling water for 2 minutes. Drain, refresh under cold running water and drain again. Cut the fennel bulbs in half and place in a large, shallow, non-metallic dish. Cut the corn cobs in half across the centre and add to the dish with the tomatoes and onions.

2 Mix the oil, lemon juice, garlic and marjoram in a jug and season to taste with salt and pepper. Pour the mixture over the vegetables, cover with clingfilm and leave to marinate for 1 hour.

3 Preheat the barbecue. Drain the vegetables, reserving the marinade. Thread the corn and cherry tomatoes alternately on to presoaked wooden skewers. Brush the peppers with oil and cook over medium hot coals, turning frequently, for 10 minutes. Add the onion and fennel to the barbecue and cook, brushing with the marinade, for 5 minutes. Turn the onion and fennel and brush with marinade. Add the skewers, brush with marinade and cook, turning and brushing frequently with more marinade, for 10 minutes. Transfer the vegetables to a large plate and serve with mayonnaise.

stuffed tomato parcels

SERVES	PREP		COOK
4	**15** mins	**+15 mins** cooling	**20** mins

An unusual filling for stuffed tomatoes, the spinach and cheese are given extra flavour with toasted sunflower seeds.

1 Preheat the barbecue. Heat the oil in a heavy-based saucepan. Add the sunflower seeds and cook, stirring constantly, for 2 minutes, or until golden. Add the onion and cook over a low heat, stirring occasionally, for 5 minutes, or until softened but not browned. Add the garlic and spinach, cover and cook for 2–3 minutes, or until the spinach has wilted. Remove the saucepan from the heat and season to taste with nutmeg, salt and pepper. Leave to cool.

2 Using a sharp knife, cut off and reserve a thin slice from the top of each tomato and scoop out the flesh with a teaspoon, taking care not to pierce the shell. Chop the flesh and stir it into the spinach mixture with the mozzarella cheese.

3 Fill the tomato shells with the spinach and cheese mixture and replace the tops. Cut 4 squares of foil, each large enough to enclose a tomato. Place one tomato in the centre of each square and fold up the sides to enclose securely. Cook over hot coals, turning occasionally, for 10 minutes. Serve immediately in the parcels.

ingredients

1 tbsp olive oil
2 tbsp sunflower seeds
1 onion, finely chopped
1 garlic clove, finely chopped
500 g/1 lb 2 oz fresh spinach, thick
  stalks removed and leaves shredded
pinch of freshly grated nutmeg
salt and pepper
4 beef tomatoes
140 g/5 oz mozzarella cheese, diced

spicy caribbean kebabs

ingredients

1 corn cob
1 christophene, peeled and
  cut into chunks
1 ripe plantain, peeled and cut
  into thick slices
1 aubergine, cut into chunks
1 red pepper, deseeded and cut
  into chunks
1 green pepper, deseeded and cut
  into chunks
1 onion, cut into wedges
8 button mushrooms
4 cherry tomatoes

marinade

150 ml/5 fl oz tomato juice
4 tbsp sunflower oil
4 tbsp lime juice
3 tbsp dark soy sauce
1 shallot, finely chopped
2 garlic cloves, finely chopped
1 fresh green chilli, deseeded and
  finely chopped
$1/2$ tsp ground cinnamon
pepper

SERVES	PREP		COOK
4	20 mins	+3hrs marinating	15 mins

Bring a taste of the tropics to your barbecue with a sizzling dish that is also suitable for vegans.

1 Using a sharp knife, remove the husks and silks from the corn cob and cut into 2.5-cm/1-inch thick slices. Blanch the christophene chunks in boiling water for 2 minutes. Drain, refresh under cold running water and drain again. Place the christophene chunks in a large bowl with the corn cob slices and the remaining ingredients.

2 Mix all the marinade ingredients together in a jug, seasoning to taste with pepper. Pour the marinade over the vegetables, tossing to coat. Cover with clingfilm and leave to marinate in the refrigerator for 3 hours.

3 Preheat the barbecue. Drain the vegetables, reserving the marinade. Thread the vegetables on to several metal skewers. Cook over hot coals, turning and brushing frequently with the reserved marinade, for 10–15 minutes. Transfer to a large serving plate and serve immediately.

vegetarian chilli burgers

SERVES
4-6

PREP
20
mins

+1hr
chilling

COOK
24-28
mins

To maximize the coriander's contribution, chop the root and stalks into the mixture as well as the leaves.

1 Cook the bulgar wheat in a saucepan of lightly salted water for 12 minutes, or until cooked. Drain and reserve.

2 Place the beans in a food processor with the chillies, garlic, spring onions, pepper, coriander and half the cheese. Using the pulse button, chop finely. Add to the cooked bulgar wheat with salt and pepper to taste. Mix well, then shape into 4–6 equal-sized burgers. Cover and leave to chill for 1 hour. Coat the burgers in the flour.

3 Lightly brush the burgers with oil. Preheat the barbecue and when hot, add the burgers and cook over medium hot coals for 5–6 minutes on each side or until piping hot.

4 Place 1–2 slices of tomato on top of each burger and sprinkle with the remaining cheese. Cook under the hot grill for 2–3 minutes, or until the cheese begins to melt. Serve.

ingredients

85 g/3 oz bulgar wheat
salt and pepper
300 g/10^1/$_2$ oz canned red kidney beans, drained and rinsed
300 g/10^1/$_2$ oz canned cannellini beans, drained
1–2 fresh red jalapeño chillies, deseeded and roughly chopped
2–3 garlic cloves
6 spring onions, roughly chopped
1 yellow pepper, deseeded, peeled and chopped
1 tbsp chopped fresh coriander
115 g/4 oz mature Cheddar cheese, grated
2 tbsp wholemeal flour
1–2 tbsp sunflower oil
1 large tomato, sliced

haloumi cheese & vegetable kebabs

SERVES 4

PREP 10 mins

+2hrs marinating

COOK 5-10 mins

Haloumi is just perfect for the barbecue and these kebabs are bursting with colour and taste.

1 Put the oil, vinegar, garlic and coriander into a large bowl. Season with salt and pepper and mix until well combined.

2 Cut the haloumi cheese into bite-sized cubes. Thread the cubes onto skewers, alternating them with whole button mushrooms, baby onions, cherry tomatoes, and courgette and red pepper chunks. When the skewers are full (leave a small space at either end), transfer them to the bowl and turn them in the mixture until they are well coated. Cover with clingfilm and place in the refrigerator to marinate for at least 2 hours.

3 When the skewers are thoroughly marinated, barbecue them over hot coals for 5–10 minutes or until they are cooked to your taste, turning them frequently and basting with the remaining marinade. Arrange the skewers on a bed of freshly cooked rice or fresh mixed salad leaves, garnish with coriander leaves and serve with fresh crusty bread.

ingredients

marinade
4 tbsp extra-virgin olive oil
2 tbsp balsamic vinegar
2 garlic cloves, finely chopped
1 tbsp chopped fresh coriander
salt and pepper

kebabs
225 g/8 oz haloumi cheese
12 button mushrooms
8 baby onions
12 cherry tomatoes
2 courgettes, cut into small
  chunks
1 red pepper, deseeded and cut
  into small chunks

to garnish
chopped fresh coriander

to serve
freshly cooked rice or salad
  leaves
fresh crusty bread

174

simplefunfruitskewersdeliciouscrunchy
heavenlydivine...

desserts

cinnamon fruit with chocolate sauce

SERVES	PREP	COOK
4	**10** mins	**10** mins

Fresh fruit kebabs are coated with spicy butter before barbecuing and are then served with an easy-to-prepare, rich chocolate sauce.

1 Preheat the barbecue. To make the sauce, break the chocolate into pieces and melt with the butter in a saucepan over a low heat. Stir in the sugar and evaporated milk and cook, stirring, until the sugar has dissolved and the sauce has thickened. Transfer to a heatproof bowl and set on the side of the barbecue to keep hot.

2 Cut the pineapple slices into chunks. Thread the pineapple chunks, kiwi fruit and strawberries alternately on to several presoaked wooden skewers. Mix the butter, cinnamon and orange juice together in a small bowl. Brush the fruit kebabs all over with the cinnamon butter.

3 Cook the kebabs over hot coals, turning and brushing frequently with any remaining cinnamon butter, for 3–5 minutes, or until golden. Just before serving, stir the vanilla essence and Kahlúa into the sauce.

ingredients

4 slices fresh pineapple
2 kiwi fruit, peeled and
  quartered
12 strawberries, hulled
1 tbsp melted unsalted butter
1 tsp ground cinnamon
1 tbsp orange juice

sauce
225 g/8 oz plain chocolate
25 g/1 oz unsalted butter
125 g/4^1/$_2$ oz caster sugar
125 ml/4 fl oz evaporated milk
1 tsp vanilla essence
4 tbsp Kahlúa

179

ingredients

pineapple
tbsp dark rum
tbsp muscovado sugar
tsp ground ginger
tbsp unsalted butter, melted

totally tropical pineapple

SERVES
4

PREP
15
mins

COOK
6-8
mins

As this succulent dessert is cooking the delicious aroma of fresh pineapple will transport you to a Caribbean beach.

1 Preheat the barbecue. Using a sharp knife, cut off the crown of the pineapple, then cut the fruit into 2-cm/¾-inch thick slices. Cut away the peel from each slice and flick out the 'eyes' with the point of the knife. Stamp out the cores with an apple corer or small pastry cutter.

2 Mix the rum, sugar, ginger and butter together in a jug, stirring constantly, until the sugar has dissolved. Brush the pineapple rings with the rum mixture.

3 Cook the pineapple rings over hot coals for 3–4 minutes on each side. Transfer to serving plates and serve immediately with the remaining rum mixture poured over them.

baked bananas

SERVES	PREP	COOK
4	**30** mins	**10** mins

The orange-flavoured cream can be prepared in advance but do not make up the banana parcels until just before you need to cook them.

1 Preheat the barbecue. To make the orange-flavoured cream, pour the double cream into a mixing bowl and sprinkle over the icing sugar. Whisk the mixture until it is standing in soft peaks. Carefully fold in the orange-flavoured liqueur and chill in the refrigerator until required.

2 Peel the bananas and place each one on a sheet of kitchen foil.

3 Cut the passion fruit in half and squeeze the juice of each half over each banana. Spoon over the orange juice and liqueur.

4 Fold the kitchen foil over the top of the bananas so that they are completely enclosed.

5 Place the parcels on a grilling rack and barbecue the bananas over medium hot coals for about 10 minutes or until they are just tender (test by inserting a cocktail stick).

6 Transfer the foil parcels to warm, individual serving plates. Open out the foil parcels at the table and then serve immediately with the chilled orange-flavoured cream.

ingredients

4 bananas
2 passion fruit
4 tbsp orange juice
4 tbsp orange-flavoured liqueur

orange flavoured cream
150 ml/5 fl oz double cream
3 tbsp icing sugar
2 tbsp orange-flavoured liqueur

panettone with mascarpone & strawberries

SERVES **4**

PREP **10** mins

+30 mins chilling

COOK **5** mins

Panettone is a sweet Italian fruit bread. It is delicious toasted and topped with marscapone cheese and marinated strawberries.

1 Hull and slice the strawberries and place them in a bowl. Add the sugar, Marsala and cinnamon to the strawberries.

2 Toss the strawberries in the sugar and cinnamon mixture until they are well coated. Leave to chill in the refrigerator for at least 30 minutes.

3 Preheat the barbecue. When ready to serve, transfer the slices of panettone to a rack set over medium hot coals. Cook the panettone for 1 minute on each side, or until golden brown.

4 Remove the panettone from the barbecue and transfer to serving plates. Top the panettone with the mascarpone cheese and the marinated strawberries. Serve immediately.

ingredients

225 g/8 oz strawberries
25 g/1 oz caster sugar
6 tbsp Marsala wine
$^1/_2$ tsp ground cinnamon
4 slices panettone
4 tbsp mascarpone cheese

crunchy ginger apples

ingredients

4 crisp, tart apples
2 tbsp lemon juice
2 tbsp butter, melted
2 tbsp demerara sugar
4 tbsp diced stem ginger

to serve
crème fraîche
whipped cream
ice cream

to decorate
mint leaves

SERVES	PREP	COOK
4	5 mins	10 mins

Good crunchy apples and the kick of ginger is wonderfully complemented by the coolness of ice cream or crème fraîche.

1 Cut the apples in half through their circumference. Carefully remove the pips and core. Preheat the barbecue.

2 Place the lemon juice, butter and demerara sugar in three separate small dishes. Dip the cut side of the apples first in the lemon juice, then in the melted butter and, finally, in the sugar.

3 Cook the apples, cut side down over medium-hot coals for 5 minutes or until the sugar caramelises and the apple softens slightly. Turn and cook for an additional 5 minutes to blacken the skin. The cooked apples should still retain their crunch.

4 Arrange the apple halves in individual dishes (allowing two halves per serving), cut side up, and spoon diced ginger over each half. Decorate with mint leaves and serve with a bowl of crème fraîche, whipped cream or ice cream.

stuffed pears

SERVES **4** PREP **20** mins COOK **20** mins

ingredients

2 tsp unsalted butter,
  for greasing
4 firm dessert pears
2 tbsp lemon juice
4 tbsp rosehip syrup
1 tsp green peppercorns,
  lightly crushed
140 g/5 oz redcurrants
4 tbsp caster sugar

to serve
ice cream

It is a popular practice to sprinkle strawberries with pepper to bring out their flavour — this is equally effective with other fruit.

1 Preheat the barbecue. Cut out 4 squares of foil, each large enough to enclose the pears, and grease with the butter. Halve and core the pears, but do not peel. Brush the cut surfaces with lemon juice. Place 2 pear halves on each of the foil squares, brush them with the rosehip syrup and sprinkle with the peppercorns.

2 Place the redcurrants in a bowl and sprinkle with the sugar. Spoon the redcurrant mixture into the cavities of the pears. Fold up the sides of the foil to enclose the pears securely.

3 Cook over hot coals for 20 minutes. Serve immediately with ice cream.

fruity skewers with chocolate dip

SERVES	PREP	COOK
4	**20** mins	**10-15** mins

These warm, lightly barbecued fruit kebabs are served with a delicious chocolate dipping sauce.

1 Preheat the barbecue. To make the chocolate dip, place the butter, chocolate, cocoa powder and golden syrup in a small saucepan. Heat gently on a hob or at the side of the barbecue, stirring constantly, until all of the ingredients have melted and are well combined.

2 To prepare the fruit, peel and core as necessary, then cut into large, bite-sized pieces or wedges as appropriate. Dip apples, pears and bananas in lemon juice to prevent discoloration. Thread the pieces of fruit on to several metal skewers.

3 Mix the honey, orange juice and rind together. Heat gently if required and brush over the fruit.

4 Cook the fruit skewers over warm coals for 5–10 minutes, until hot, brushing on more glaze. Serve with the chocolate dip.

ingredients

selection of fruit – choose from
oranges, bananas, strawberries,
pineapple chunks, apricots,
dessert apples, pears, kiwi fruit
1 tbsp lemon juice
6 tbsp clear honey
grated rind and juice of
1/2 orange

chocolate dip
30 g/1¼ oz butter
50 g/1¾ oz plain chocolate,
broken into small cubes
1/2 tbsp cocoa powder
2 tbsp golden syrup

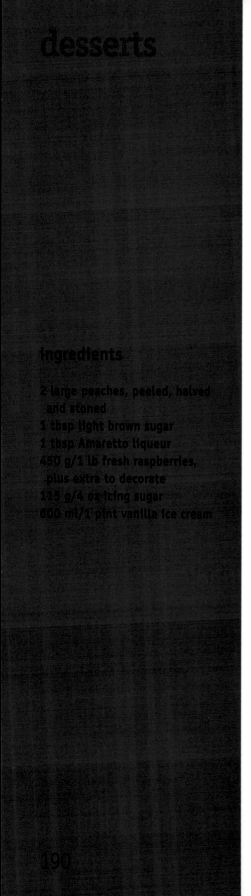

ingredients

2 large peaches, peeled, halved
 and stoned
1 tbsp light brown sugar
1 tbsp Amaretto liqueur
450 g/1 lb fresh raspberries,
 plus extra to decorate
115 g/4 oz icing sugar
600 ml/1 pint vanilla ice cream

special peach melba

SERVES	PREP		COOK
4	**15** mins	**+15 mins** marinating	**3-5** hours

The elegant simplicity of this rich, fruity dessert makes it the perfect end to a special occasion barbecue party.

1 Place the peach halves in a large, shallow dish and sprinkle with the brown sugar. Pour the Amaretto liqueur over them, cover with clingfilm and leave to marinate for 1 hour.

2 Meanwhile, using the back of a spoon, press the raspberries through a fine sieve set over a bowl. Discard the contents of the sieve. Stir the icing sugar into the raspberry purée. Cover the bowl with clingfilm and leave to chill in the refrigerator until required.

3 Preheat the barbecue. Drain the peach halves, reserving the marinade. Cook over hot coals, turning and brushing frequently with the reserved marinade, for 3–5 minutes. To serve, put 2 scoops of vanilla ice cream in each of 4 sundae glasses, top with a peach half and spoon the raspberry sauce over it. Decorate with whole raspberries and serve.

exotic fruity parcels

SERVES
4

PREP
20
mins

+30 mins
marinating

COOK
20
mins

Delicious pieces of exotic fruit are warmed through in a deliciously scented sauce to make a fabulous barbecue dessert.

1 Cut the papaya in half, scoop out the seeds and discard them. Peel the papaya and cut the flesh into thick slices.

2 Prepare the mango by cutting it lengthwise in half either side of the central stone.

3 Score each mango half in a criss-cross pattern. Push each mango half inside out to separate the cubes and cut them away from the peel.

4 Using a sharp knife, thickly slice the star fruit. Place all of the fruit in a bowl and mix them together.

5 Mix the grenadine and orange juice together and pour over the fruit. Leave to marinate for at least 30 minutes.

6 Divide the fruit among 4 double thickness squares of kitchen foil and gather up the edges to form a parcel that encloses the fruit.

7 Place the foil parcel on a rack set over warm coals and barbecue the fruit for 15–20 minutes.

8 Serve the fruit in the parcel, with single cream or yogurt offered separately.

ingredients

1 papaya
1 mango
1 star fruit
1 tbsp grenadine
3 tbsp orange juice

to serve
single cream or
natural yogurt

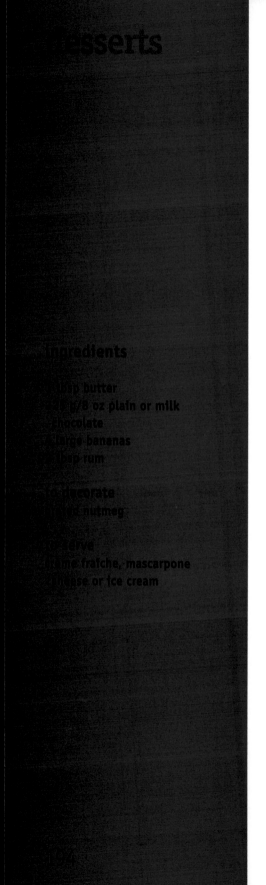

ingredients

1 tbsp butter
250 g/8 oz plain or milk
chocolate
4 large bananas
4 tbsp rum

to decorate
grated nutmeg

to serve
crème fraîche, mascarpone
cheese or ice cream

chocolate rum bananas

SERVES 4   **PREP 5 mins**   **COOK 10 mins**

Bananas are very sweet when barbecued, and conveniently come in their own protective wrapping.

1 Take four 25-cm/10-inch squares of aluminium foil and brush them with butter.

2 Cut the chocolate into very small pieces. Make a careful slit lengthways in the peel of each banana, and open just wide enough to insert the chocolate. Place the chocolate pieces inside the bananas, along their lengths, then close them up.

3 Wrap each stuffed banana in a square of foil, then barbecue them over hot coals for about 5–10 minutes, or until the chocolate has melted inside the bananas. Remove from the barbecue, place the bananas on individual serving plates and pour some rum into each banana.

4 Serve at once with crème fraîche, mascarpone cheese or ice cream, topped with nutmeg.

caramelized fruit medley

SERVES	PREP		COOK
4	**10** mins	**+2hrs** marinating	**8** mins

Grilling fruit brings out its full flavour and makes it simply irresistible on a summer's evening.

1 Cut the pineapple into thick slices across. Cut off the peel with a small sharp knife, then, holding each slice upright, cut out the 'eyes'. Stamp out the core from each slice with an apple corer. Halve the melon and scoop out the seeds with a teaspoon. Cut into thick wedges and peel with a sharp knife.

2 Mix the sherry and sugar together in a large dish, stirring until the sugar has dissolved. Add all the fruit and toss well to coat. Cover and leave to marinate in a cool place for 2 hours.

3 Drain the fruit, reserving the marinade. Grill the pineapple on a hot barbecue for 4 minutes, then turn over and brush with the marinade. Add the melon and grill for 2 minutes, then turn over and brush with the marinade. Add the strawberries and grill for 2 minutes. By this time, the fruit should all be golden and juicy. Serve immediately.

ingredients

1 fresh pineapple
1 Ogen melon
150 ml/5 fl oz sweet sherry
115 g/4 oz caster sugar
225 g/8 oz large strawberries

dipsmarinadescrispysaladgarlicbreadsharing
temptingaccompaniments...

sides, sauces & salads

crispy potato skins

SERVES	PREP	COOK
4-6	**10** mins	**1hr 20** mins

Use the potato flesh in this recipe for another meal, so make slightly more than you think you need.

1 Preheat the oven to 200°C/400°F/Gas Mark 6. Prick the potatoes with a fork and bake for 1 hour, or until tender. Alternatively, cook in a microwave on high for 12–15 minutes. Cut the potatoes in half and scoop out the flesh, leaving about 5 mm/¼ inch potato flesh lining the skin.

2 Preheat the barbecue. Brush the insides of the potato with melted butter.

3 Place the skins, cut-side down, over medium hot coals and cook for 10–15 minutes. Turn the potato skins over and barbecue for a further 5 minutes, or until they are crispy. Take care that they do not burn. Season the potato skins with salt and pepper to taste and serve while they are still warm.

4 If wished, the skins can be filled with a variety of toppings. Barbecue the potato skins as above for 10 minutes, then turn cut-side up and sprinkle with slices of spring onion, grated cheese and chopped salami. Barbecue for a further 5 minutes, or until the cheese begins to melt. Serve hot.

ingredients

8 small baking potatoes, scrubbed
50 g/1³/₄ oz butter, melted
salt and pepper

optional topping
6 spring onions, sliced
50 g/1³/₄ oz grated Gruyère cheese
50 g/1³/₄ oz salami, cut into thin strips

garlic bread

SERVES	PREP	COOK
6	**10** mins	**15** mins

ingredients

150 g/5¹/₂ oz butter, softened
3 cloves garlic, crushed
2 tbsp chopped, fresh parsley
pepper
1 large or 2 small sticks of
   French bread

A perennial favourite, garlic bread is perfect with a range of barbecue meals.

1 Mix together the butter, garlic and parsley in a bowl until well combined. Season with pepper to taste and mix well.

2 Cut the French bread into thick slices.

3 Spread the flavoured butter over one side of each slice and reassemble the loaf on a large sheet of thick kitchen foil.

4 Wrap the bread well and barbecue over hot coals for 10–15 minutes until the butter melts and the bread is piping hot.

5 Serve as an accompaniment to a wide range of dishes.

home-made oven chips

SERVES
4

PREP
10
mins

COOK
40-45
mins

The perfect barbecue accompaniment, you are sure to be popular with these tasty home-made chips.

1 Preheat the oven to 200°C/400°F/Gas Mark 6.

2 Cut the potatoes into thick, even-sized chips. Rinse them under cold running water and then dry well on a clean tea towel. Put in a bowl, add the oil and toss together until coated.

3 Spread the chips on a baking sheet and cook in the oven for 40–45 minutes, turning once, until golden. Add salt and pepper to taste and serve hot.

ingredients

450 g/1 lb potatoes, peeled
2 tbsp sunflower oil
salt and pepper

potato fans

SERVES	PREP	COOK
6	**5** mins	**1** hr

ingredients

6 large potatoes, scrubbed but
  not peeled
2 tbsp garlic-flavoured olive oil

**These garlic-flavoured potatoes are baked in foil on the barbecue.
They need plenty of time to cook.**

1 Make a series of cuts across the potatoes almost all the way
through. Cut out 6 squares of foil, each large enough to
enclose a potato.

2 Place a potato on each square of foil and brush generously
with the garlic-flavoured oil. Fold up the sides to enclose the
potatoes entirely.

3 Cook on a hot barbecue, turning occasionally, for 1 hour.
To serve, open the foil parcels and gently pinch the potatoes
to open up the fans.

pepper salad

SERVES	PREP	COOK
4	5-10 mins	35 mins

Colourful marinated Mediterranean vegetables make a tasty starter, especially when served with fresh bread or Tomato Toasts.

1 Cut the onion into wedges. Core and deseed the peppers and cut into thick slices.

2 Heat the oil in a heavy-based frying pan. Add the onion, peppers, courgettes and garlic and cook gently for 20 minutes, stirring occasionally.

3 Add the vinegar, anchovies, olives and seasoning to taste, mix thoroughly and leave to cool. Spoon the cooled mixture on to individual plates and sprinkle with the basil.

4 To make the Tomato Toasts, preheat the oven to 220°C/425°F/Gas Mark 7. Cut the French bread diagonally into 1-cm/½-inch slices. Mix the garlic, tomato, oil and seasoning together, and spread thinly over each slice of bread.

5 Place the bread on a baking tray and bake in the preheated oven for 5–10 minutes, until crisp. Serve with the vegetable salad.

ingredients

1 onion
2 red peppers
2 yellow peppers
3 tbsp olive oil
2 large courgettes, sliced
2 garlic cloves, sliced
1 tbsp balsamic vinegar
50 g/1³/₄ oz anchovy fillets, chopped
25 g/1 oz black olives, halved and stoned
salt and pepper
1 tbsp chopped fresh basil

tomato toasts
small stick of French bread
1 garlic clove, crushed
1 tomato, peeled and chopped
2 tbsp olive oil
salt and pepper

pasta salad with basil vinaigrette

SERVES
4

PREP
20
mins

COOK
12-15
mins

All the ingredients of pesto sauce are included in this salad, which has a fabulous summery taste, perfect for alfresco eating.

1 Cook the pasta in a large saucepan of lightly salted boiling water for 10–12 minutes, or until just tender but still firm to the bite. Drain the pasta, rinse under cold running water, then drain again thoroughly. Place the pasta in a large bowl.

2 Preheat the grill to medium. To make the vinaigrette, place the basil leaves, garlic, cheese, olive oil and lemon juice in a food processor. Season to taste with salt and pepper and process until the leaves are well chopped and the ingredients are combined. Alternatively, finely chop the basil leaves by hand and combine with the other vinaigrette ingredients. Pour the vinaigrette over the pasta and toss to coat.

3 Cut the tomatoes into wedges. Stone and halve the olives. Slice the sun-dried tomatoes. Toast the pine kernels on a baking tray under the hot grill until golden.

4 Add the tomatoes (fresh and sun-dried) and the olives to the pasta and mix until combined.

5 Transfer the pasta to a serving dish, sprinkle over the Parmesan and toasted pine kernels and serve garnished with a few basil leaves.

ingredients

225 g/8 oz dried fusilli
salt and pepper
4 tomatoes
50 g/1³/₄ oz black olives
25 g/1 oz sun-dried tomatoes in oil
2 tbsp pine kernels
2 tbsp freshly grated Parmesan
  cheese

to garnish
fresh basil leaves

vinaigrette
15 g/¹/₂ oz basil leaves
1 garlic clove, crushed
2 tbsp freshly grated Parmesan
  cheese
4 tbsp extra-virgin olive oil
2 tbsp lemon juice

moroccan spiced salad

ingredients

2 tbsp olive oil
90 g/3¹/₄ oz long-grain rice
400 ml/14 fl oz water
4 tbsp lemon-flavoured or
  extra-virgin olive oil
3 tbsp vinegar
1 tbsp lemon juice
1 tbsp honey
1 tsp garam masala
1 tsp ground coriander
¹/₂ tsp mustard
225 g/8 oz canned red kidney beans
225 g/8 oz canned chickpeas
2 shallots, chopped
4 spring onions, trimmed and sliced
60 g/2¹/₄ oz pine kernels
100 g/3¹/₂ oz sultanas
1 tbsp chopped fresh mint

to garnish
chopped fresh mint

to serve
wedges of fresh lemon

SERVES	PREP	COOK
4	15 mins	40 mins

This superb salad is great for vegetarians and non-vegetarians alike, full of flavour, texture and healthy foods.

1 Heat the olive oil in a large saucepan. Add the rice and cook for 3 minutes, stirring, over a low heat. Pour in the water and bring to the boil, then lower the heat, cover and simmer for 35 minutes. Remove from the heat and transfer to a colander. Rinse under cold running water, drain well and set aside to cool.

2 In a large bowl, mix together the lemon-flavoured oil or extra-virgin olive oil, vinegar, lemon juice and honey. Add the garam masala, coriander and mustard and stir well.

3 Add the rice and mix well. Rinse and drain the kidney beans and chickpeas, then add them to the bowl with the shallots, spring onions, pine kernels, sultanas and mint. Divide the salad between serving bowls, garnish with chopped fresh mint and serve with lemon wedges.

avocado salad with lime dressing

SERVES	PREP	COOK
4	20 mins	0 mins

This salad must be served fresh to prevent discolouration and floppy salad leaves.

1 Wash and drain the lettuce and rocket, if necessary. Shred all the leaves and arrange in the bottom of a large salad bowl. Add the spring onions, tomatoes and walnuts.

2 Halve, peel and stone the avocados and cut into thin slices or small chunks. Brush with the lemon juice to prevent discolouration, then transfer to the salad bowl. Mix together gently.

3 Put the dressing ingredients into a screw-top jar, screw on the lid tightly and shake well until thoroughly combined. Drizzle the dressing over the salad and serve immediately.

ingredients

60 g/2^1/$_4$ oz mixed fresh red
  and green lettuce leaves
60 g/2^1/$_4$ oz fresh wild rocket
4 spring onions, finely diced
5 tomatoes, sliced
25 g/1 oz walnuts, toasted
  and chopped
2 avocados
1 tbsp lemon juice

lime dressing
1 tbsp lime juice
1 tsp French mustard
1 tbsp crème fraîche
1 tbsp chopped fresh parsley or
  coriander
3 tbsp extra-virgin olive oil
pinch of sugar
salt and pepper

salade niçoise

SERVES 4

PREP 12–15 mins

COOK 13–17 mins

This Provençal dish is probably the best-known and best-loved classic salad in the Western world.

1 Cook the eggs, potatoes and beans simultaneously. Place the eggs in a saucepan and cover with cold water. Bring to the boil, then reduce the heat and boil gently for 12 minutes. Cook the potatoes in a saucepan of lightly salted boiling water for 12–15 minutes, or until tender, and cook the green beans in a separate saucepan of lightly salted boiling water for 3–5 minutes.

2 Meanwhile, prepare all the remaining ingredients. Roughly chop the lettuces, drain and flake the tuna, then drain the anchovies and halve them lengthways. Chop the tomatoes and slice the spring onions. To make the dressing, place all the ingredients in a large salad bowl and beat well to mix.

3 Drain the beans and refresh in cold water. Add to the salad bowl with the lettuces, tuna, anchovies, tomatoes, spring onions, olives and capers. Drain the eggs, cool under cold running water and reserve. Drain the potatoes and add to the salad. Lightly toast the pine kernels in a dry frying pan, shaking the frying pan frequently, for 1–2 minutes, or until golden. Sprinkle them over the salad. Shell and chop the eggs and add them to the salad.

4 Whisk the dressing again, add it to the salad, toss to coat and serve.

ingredients

2 eggs
12 small salad potatoes, such as Pink Fir Apple or Maris Bard
salt
115 g/4 oz green beans
2 cos lettuces or 3 Little Gem lettuces
200 g/7 oz canned tuna in oil
6 canned anchovy fillets
4 tomatoes
4 spring onions
12 black olives
2 tbsp bottled capers, drained
2 tbsp pine kernels

dressing
6 tbsp extra-virgin olive oil
2 tbsp tarragon vinegar
1 tsp Dijon mustard
1 garlic clove, finely chopped

sweet & sour marinade

SERVES	PREP	COOK
4	5 mins	0 mins

Sweet and sour is a classic taste combination and will always be popular.

1 Combine the fruit juice, sherry, soy sauce, chicken stock and cider vinegar in a mixing bowl.

2 Stir in the tomato purée, sugar, garlic and ginger. Mix well.

3 This mixture can be used to marinate and baste chicken or pork.

ingredients

225 ml/8 fl oz orange,
 grapefruit or pineapple juice
2 tbsp sweet sherry
125 ml/4 fl oz dark soy sauce
125 ml/4 fl oz chicken stock
50 ml/2 fl oz cider vinegar
1 tbsp tomato purée
55 g/2 oz light brown sugar
1 tsp powdered garlic
1 tsp powdered ginger

ingredients

2 garlic cloves, crushed
1 tsp salt
4 tbsp finely chopped fresh mint
225 ml/8 fl oz plain yogurt
1 tsp ground cumin, coriander
  seeds or cinnamon, optional
1 onion, optional

minted yogurt marinade

SERVES
4

PREP
10
mins

COOK
0
mins

You can prepare this marinade in advance and chill in the refrigerator until needed.

1 Mix the garlic with the salt to make a paste. Turn into a mixing bowl and stir in the mint, yogurt and cumin (or coriander or cinnamon, if using).

2 If you are using onion, place it in a food processor, together with the yogurt mixture and blend for a few seconds, or until the mixture is coarse and the onions blended in.

3 Use to marinate and baste lamb.

ingredients

4 tomatoes
1 red onion or 6 spring onions
1–2 garlic cloves, crushed
  (optional)
2 tbsp chopped fresh coriander
$^1/_2$ red or green chilli (optional)
finely grated rind of $^1/_2$–1 lemon
  or lime
1–2 tbsp lemon or lime juice
pepper

tomato salsa

SERVES	PREP	COOK
4	10 mins	0 mins

This salad is used extensively in Mexican cooking and served as a dip or a relish, and is eaten as an accompaniment to almost any dish.

1 Chop the tomatoes fairly finely and evenly, and put into a bowl. They must be firm and a good strong red colour for the best results, but if preferred, they may be peeled by placing them in boiling water for about 20 seconds and then plunging into cold water. The skins should then slip off easily when they are nicked with a knife.

2 Peel and slice the red onion thinly, or trim the spring onions and cut into thin slanting slices; add to the chopped tomatoes with the garlic and coriander and mix lightly.

3 Remove the seeds from the red or green chilli, chop the flesh very finely and add to the salad. Treat the chillies with care; do not touch your eyes or face after handling them until you have washed your hands thoroughly. Chilli juices can burn.

4 Add the lemon or lime rind and juice to the salsa, and mix well. Transfer to a serving bowl and sprinkle with pepper.

honey mustard marinade

SERVES
4

PREP
5
mins

COOK
0
mins

This sweet tangy marinade is perfect to baste meat or vegetables.

1 Combine all the ingredients except the oil in a small mixing bowl.

2 Gradually add the oil, whisking constantly, until it is fully absorbed into the mixture.

3 Use to marinate and baste chicken or pork, especially spareribs.

ingredients

2 tbsp honey
2 tbsp wholegrain mustard
1 tsp ground ginger
1 tsp garlic powder
2 tsp fresh rosemary, chopped finely
4 tbsp dark soy sauce
50 ml/2 fl oz olive oil

index

index